Collins

Cambridge Lower Secondary
English
STAGE 7: WORKBOOK

T0312377

Series editors: Julia Burchell and Mike Gould
Authors: Mike Gould, Richard Patterson,
Alison Ramage and Lucy Toop

William Collins' dream of knowledge for all began with the publication of his first book in 1819.

A self-educated mill worker, he not only enriched millions of lives, but also founded a flourishing publishing house. Today, staying true to this spirit, Collins books are packed with inspiration, innovation and practical expertise. They place you at the centre of a world of possibility and give you exactly what you need to explore it.

Collins. Freedom to teach.

Published by Collins

An imprint of HarperCollins*Publishers*

The News Building
1 London Bridge Street
London SE1 9GF

HarperCollins*Publishers*
Macken House, 39/40 Mayor Street Upper,
Dublin 1, D01 C9W8, Ireland

Browse the complete Collins catalogue at
www.collins.co.uk

© HarperCollins*Publishers* Limited 2020

10 9 8 7 6

ISBN 978-0-00-836417-5

British Library Cataloguing-in-Publication Data
A catalogue record for this publication is available from the British Library.

Third-party websites, publications and resources referred to in this publication have not been endorsed by Cambridge Assessment International Education.

With thanks to the following teachers for reviewing a sample of the Workbook in development:
Abhinandan Bhattacharya, JBCN International School Oshiwara, Mumbai, India; Preeti Roychoudhury, Calcutta International School, Calcutta, India; Priya Saxena Manthan, International School, Hyderbad, India; Judith Hughes International School of Budapest, Budapest.

Third-party websites, publications and resources referred to in this publication have not been endorsed by Cambridge Assessment International Education.

Authors: Mike Gould, Richard Patterson, Alison Ramage and Lucy Toop
Series editors: Mike Gould and Julia Burchell
Product manager: Catherine Martin
Development editor: Judith Walters
Copyeditor: Catherine Dakin
Proofreader: Sonya Newland
Cover designer: Gordon McGilp
Cover illustration: Ann Paganuzzi
Internal designer: 2Hoots Publishing Services Ltd
Production controller: Lyndsey Rogers
Printed and bound in India by
Replika Press Pvt. Ltd.

MIX
Paper | Supporting responsible forestry
FSC www.fsc.org FSC™ C007454

This book is produced from independently certified FSC™ paper to ensure responsible forest management.

For more information visit: **www.harpercollins.co.uk/green**

This book is produced from independently certified FSC™ paper to ensure responsible forest management.

For more information visit: www.harpercollins.co.uk/green

Acknowledgements
The publishers gratefully acknowledge the permission granted to reproduce the copyright material in this book. Every effort has been made to trace copyright holders and to obtain their permission for the use of copyright material. The publishers will gladly receive any information enabling them to rectify any error or omission at the first opportunity.

p14 Marso/Shutterstock, p15 myboys.me/Shutterstock, p17 Kuttelvaserova Stuchelova/Shutterstock, p21 Olga Danylenko/Shutterstock, p24 Tarcisio Schnaider/Shutterstock, p33 Daniele COSSU/Shutterstock, p42 Asian foto/Shutterstock, p44 Rawpixel.com/Shutterstock, p50 Aubord Dulac/Shutterstock, p57 GrashAlex/Shutterstock, p. 62 by Paul/Shutterstock, p68 2Hoots, p72 Zurijeta/Shutterstock, p80 AF archive/Alamy Stock Photo, p84 yhelfman/Shutterstock, p86 tlorna/Shutterstock, p88 Photoongraphy/Shutterstock, p89 Eric Isselee/Shutterstock, p90 Chokniti Khongchum/Shutterstock, p90 Vaclav Sebek/Shutterstock.

We are grateful to the following for permission to reproduce copyright material:

An extract on p.17 from *Cider* with Rosie by Laurie Lee, Chatto & Windus, copyright © Laurie Lee, 1959. Reproduced by permission of The Random House Group Ltd and Curtis Brown Ltd, London on behalf of The Beneficiaries of the Estate of Laurie Lee; and an extract on p.56 from *The Tall Woman and Her Short Husband* by Feng Ji-cai, published in *Contemporary Chinese Fiction*, 2006, copyright © 1998, pp.238–239. Reproduced with permission of the Licensor through PLSclear; and Penguin Random House LLC.

Contents

Introduction   4

Key features of the Workbook   5

Chapter 1 Describing: A sense of place   6

Chapter 2 Informing: Our environment   21

Chapter 3 Advising and persuading: Animals in captivity   37

Chapter 4 Narrating: Mystery and suspense stories   54

Chapter 5 Reviewing and discussing: Plays about outsiders   68

Chapter 6 Exploring and commenting: Animal poetry   84

Introduction

The Collins *Stage 7 Student's Book* and *Workbook* offer a rich programme of skills development, based on a varied and stimulating set of texts and tasks, designed to match the Cambridge Lower Secondary English curriculum framework.

The *Stage 7 Workbook* directly supports the Student's Book, with a Workbook unit for nearly every unit in Chapters 1 to 6 of the Student's Book. The units are numbered in the same way to make the link between the two resources clear.

The Workbook units give you the opportunity to consolidate your learning through further practice of the skills taught in the Student's Book. Often, they provide extra support and reinforce key points of grammar or language.

Workbook tasks are scaffolded and broken into manageable steps to enable you to complete them by yourself for self-study or homework, if your teacher decides that is appropriate. Many tasks can be completed in the Workbook itself; longer tasks will need to be completed in your exercise book or on paper.

Answers are provided in the *Stage 7 Teacher's Guide*.

You will notice there is no Workbook unit in each chapter that corresponds to the 'Enjoy reading' unit at the start of the Student's Book chapter. That unit was all about reading a longer text and sharing your first impressions of it with your classmates through discussion. If you wanted to extend that experience in your own time, you could find an example of another text written for the same purpose and ask yourself the same kinds of questions about it.

In the Workbook units, you will read more fascinating texts from different cultures and eras, written in a range of forms and genres. You will also be asked to write a wide variety of texts yourself, learning from the texts and writers you are reading. And your speaking and listening skills will be supported through planning and reflection tasks.

Each chapter ends with two substantial final tasks to help you apply your learning: one longer writing task, and one set of final reading tasks responding to a longer text.

We hope our skills-building approach helps you and your teachers to fulfil the demands of your English course in an enjoyable and enriching way.

Julia Burchell and **Mike Gould**, Series Editors

Key features of the Workbook

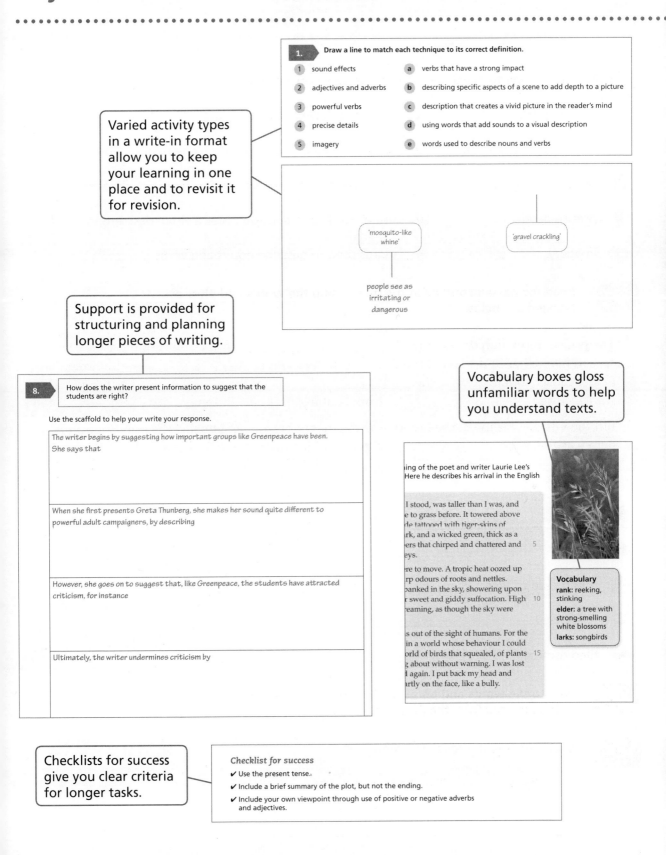

1. ▶ Draw a line to match each technique to its correct definition.

1. sound effects
2. adjectives and adverbs
3. powerful verbs
4. precise details
5. imagery

a. verbs that have a strong impact
b. describing specific aspects of a scene to add depth to a picture
c. description that creates a vivid picture in the reader's mind
d. using words that add sounds to a visual description
e. words used to describe nouns and verbs

> Varied activity types in a write-in format allow you to keep your learning in one place and to revisit it for revision.

'mosquito-like whine'

'gravel crackling'

people see as irritating or dangerous

> Support is provided for structuring and planning longer pieces of writing.

8. ▶ How does the writer present information to suggest that the students are right?

Use the scaffold to help your write your response.

The writer begins by suggesting how important groups like Greenpeace have been. She says that

When she first presents Greta Thunberg, she makes her sound quite different to powerful adult campaigners, by describing

However, she goes on to suggest that, like Greenpeace, the students have attracted criticism, for instance

Ultimately, the writer undermines criticism by

> Vocabulary boxes gloss unfamiliar words to help you understand texts.

...ing of the poet and writer Laurie Lee's ... Here he describes his arrival in the English

... I stood, was taller than I was, and ... e to grass before. It towered above ... de tattooed with tiger-skins of ... rk, and a wicked green, thick as a ... ers that chirped and chattered and   5 ... eys.

... re to move. A tropic heat oozed up ... rp odours of roots and nettles. ... banked in the sky, showering upon ... r sweet and giddy suffocation. High   10 ... eaming, as though the sky were

... s out of the sight of humans. For the ... in a world whose behaviour I could ... rld of birds that squealed, of plants   15 ... g about without warning. I was lost ... again. I put back my head and ... rtly on the face, like a bully.

Vocabulary
rank: reeking, stinking
elder: a tree with strong-smelling white blossoms
larks: songbirds

> Checklists for success give you clear criteria for longer tasks.

Checklist for success
✔ Use the present tense.
✔ Include a brief summary of the plot, but not the ending.
✔ Include your own viewpoint through use of positive or negative adverbs and adjectives.

What is descriptive writing?

1. Draw a line to match each technique to its correct definition.

1. sound effects   a. verbs that have a strong impact

2. adjectives and adverbs   b. describing specific aspects of a scene to add depth to a picture

3. powerful verbs   c. description that creates a vivid picture in the reader's mind

4. precise details   d. using words that add sounds to a visual description

5. imagery   e. words used to describe nouns and verbs

2. Read the passage and fill in the gaps, using the words and phrases labelled a–e below.

The house stood high on the hillside, _____ in shadow, but the valley lay spread before her in the last of the day's light, the river a _____ among the fields. Closer, looking down, the _____ of the village glowed crimson and smoke curled _____ from cooking fires and chimneys.

But the village was too far below to hear the inevitable evening bustle: the only sound up here was the _____ of trees and the faint rasp of crickets.

a. whisper   _____

b. lazily   _____

c. thin thread of silver _____

d. swallowed   _____

e. tiled rooftops   _____

3. Next to the words and phrases labelled a–e above, write the technique used from the list in Question 1.

4. Now complete the following sentence:

When the writer describes the 'whisper of trees', it makes the wind sound _____

_____

Understanding how writers use language for effect

1. Which type of imagery is being used in each of the following examples: simile, metaphor, or personification?

a The stars were dancing heel and toe. _____

b The stars glittered like diamonds. _____

c The stars are diamonds in the sky. _____

2. Look at how one student describes the effect of imagery in Question 1b.

The writer makes the stars sound incredibly bright by using a _____: 'glittered like diamonds'. Comparing stars to gems suggests they sparkle in the night sky, and the word 'glittered' emphasises this.

a Add in the correct type of imagery to the student's response and then label the following features.

the main idea   supporting quotation   explanation of quotation

b Complete this sentence describing the effect of the image used in Question 1c.

The writer makes the stars sound precious by saying that the stars 'are' diamonds. This _____ is effective, because diamonds are _____

_____

3. Now write your own short explanation of this description, remembering to refer to the technique used.

The tired house leaned against the hill beneath its sagging roof.

_____

_____

_____

Understanding how writers create atmosphere

1. Complete the missing words in this sentence.

Writers try to capture the atmosphere or m_____d of a place, in order to give the reader a sense of what it would f_____ l_____ to be there.

2. Look at the descriptive word groups in the table. Suggest what kind of place a writer might describe and what kind of mood they might create with each group.

Description	Possible place	Mood(s)
moonlight – creaking – shadowy – padding silently		
shrieks – splash of water – coconut-scented breeze		
horns beeping – fumes – dusty		

In Workbook Unit 1.2, you looked at vocabulary in a short passage. Now read the next part of the passage, focusing on the *atmosphere* the writer has created.

But the village was too far below to hear the inevitable evening bustle: the only sound up here was the whisper of trees and the faint rasp of crickets. Occasionally, a bird called from the woods beyond the house. Sima pressed her toes into the damp grass beneath her bare feet. A lone blade tickled her instep, and she fought the urge to scratch, wanting to preserve the evening's stillness as long as possible. She closed her eyes and listened, and the air cooled around her.

She did not know how long she had stood there when she became aware of the mosquito-like whine of an engine, drawing closer. Soon, she knew, her father's car would turn into the driveway, gravel crackling beneath its tyres, shattering the peace.

Reluctantly, Sima opened her eyes.

3. Underline and label examples of language that engages the reader's senses in the passage, using the letters below.

a sight   **b** hearing   **c** touch   **d** taste   **e** smell

4. Are these statements true or false? Circle the correct letter for each statement.

a The writer suggests that Sima feels scared, alone in the garden.　T / F

b The garden is presented as a peaceful place to be.　T / F

c The mood changes when Sima realises her father will soon be home.　T / F

d The writer implies that Sima will be pleased to see her father.　T / F

5. **At the beginning of the passage, the writer creates a peaceful atmosphere in the garden. However, the language in paragraph 2 suggests that this will change when Sima's father comes home.**

a Use the spider diagrams below to gather ideas about the *implicit* meanings of these descriptions.

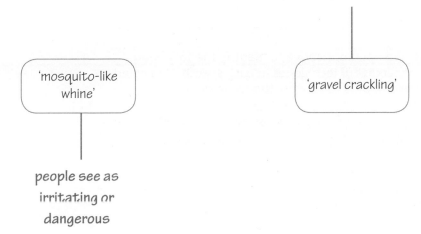

'mosquito-like whine'

'gravel crackling'

people see as irritating or dangerous

b Using one of the quotations above, explain how the writer changes the mood.

In paragraph 2, the writer makes the setting sound _____

_____

This is shown by the phrase _____

_____

The word _____

_____

Talking about important places

Read these two openings to a speech describing a visit to the market.

Speech 1

Yesterday, we went to the market to buy food for a party to celebrate a local festival. The market is a nice place, so I was happy to go along. Everyone argued over what we should buy but we agreed in the end. We bought the following: meat for the main dish, vegetables, fruit for pudding, and some nice sweets.

Speech 2

The market is one of my favourite places to visit, especially when it's festival time. Stepping into its bustle is like stepping through a wall of sounds into another world. Just walking among the stalls piled high with delicious fruit and colourful sweets, the air zinging with spices, is enough to make my mouth water.

1.

a Which speech gives you a better picture of the market? Why?

_____

_____

b Annotate the two openings above to identify the following unsuccessful or successful techniques in each speech. You could use five different colours to identify the techniques.

> powerful vocabulary   description of the senses   detail
> use of descriptive techniques   unvaried vocabulary

c Write down one thing that is included in Speech 1 that is not relevant to a description of the market.

_____

_____

2. **Now, on a separate piece of paper, write an engaging and descriptive introduction to a talk entitled 'The Delights of a Family Meal'. Include the following:**

☐ varied adjectives and adverbs

☐ powerful verbs

☐ description of the senses (sights, sounds, smells, tastes, textures)

☐ at least one descriptive technique, e.g. simile, personification.

When you have finished, check your work and tick off what you have included. How did you do?

Choosing vocabulary for effect in descriptive writing

1. Read the following paragraph. The verb 'eat' is used six times. Replace the repetitions with an appropriate alternative from the box below.

> chewing   devour   consume   munching   nibble

> After they had made me eat the green jelly, they put another plate in front of me. On the **plate** were pieces of something that were black and hard. Very cautiously I started to eat (_____) one of them, a little at a time. It was **nice** – it tasted like everything beautiful in the world. I began to eat (_____) them faster and faster, **putting** as many into my mouth as I could and eating (_____) hard to get as much of the **nice** taste as I could. I continued eating (_____) these until I was so happy, I just couldn't eat (_____) any more. Then I fell into a deep sleep.

2. Use a dictionary to find some more interesting alternatives for each of the bold words in the paragraph above.

a plate _____

b nice _____

c putting _____

3.

a Sequence these adjectives from smallest to largest.

> gigantic   small   tiny   big   medium-sized   huge   minute

_____

_____

b Now use the adjectives appropriately in the following sentences.

i) Although all the dolls were _____, the last one was so _____ you could barely see it.

ii) The mountain towered above them, so _____ that its summit was hidden in cloud.

iii) The food portions were not too filling, being _____.

4. Plan a description of a sight or something you've seen on a journey (it could be positive or negative), making sure you vary the vocabulary to describe the different senses.

How it looks: _____

_____

How it sounds: _____

_____

How it smells: _____

_____

How it feels: _____

_____

Think back to the work you did on atmosphere (Workbook Unit 1.4), then read the passage below.

> The sea **stretched out, tranquil** beneath the sky. Its **blue** depths were **crystal clear**, and **smooth as glass**. As I watched from the shore, **gentle** waves **caressed** the sand, and the **breeze whispered** in my ear.

5.

a How would you describe the mood of this passage? _____

b This description engages the senses. Draw lines to match each sense to the correct description.

hearing	caressed
touch	whispered
sight	crystal clear

c Now write your own additional sentence that uses the sense of taste.

_____

_____

d Rewrite the passage, changing the words in bold to alter the mood in the spaces below. You could make the mood miserable, stormy or exhilarating – you choose!

The sea _____, _____ beneath the sky. Its _____ depths were _____ and _____. As I watched from the shore, _____ waves _____ the sand, and the _____ _____ in my ear.

Varying sentences in descriptive writing

1. Label each sentence with the correct name: simple, compound or complex.

a Listening at the door, I heard low voices within, but I was too nervous to enter after the morning's dramatic events. _____

b Behind the door, voices muttered. _____

c I opened the door and the voices stopped abruptly. _____

2. In each of the sentences in Question 1, circle the main information (main clause) and underline the extra detail or information (subclauses).

3. Read this passage and answer the questions below.

Through the tall, iron gates, I could see the house at the end of a very long and overgrown drive [1]. It was not as big as I had thought it was going to be, but it had an impressive grandeur [2]. The roof was covered in the typical red terracotta tiles that I had seen in buildings all over the island [3]. Each window was flanked by dark green wooden shutters [4]. It was clear these had been recently painted, because they gleamed in the strong midday sun [5]. Most imposing of all was the door, its dark, polished wood dwarfed by the stone columns on either side [6]. I began to feel nervous [7].

a Write down the five words that make up the main clause (the central meaning) of the first sentence.

_____

b What kind of sentence is the second sentence [2], and what is the conjunction that signals this?

_____

c What kind of sentence is the fifth sentence [5], and what is the conjunction that signals this?

_____

d In the text, find, underline and number the phrases that add information about the following: **i** the roof tiles; **ii** the dark green shutters; **iii** the door.

e   What is the effect of using a simple sentence at the end of
    the passage?

_____

_____

4.   **Now read this passage. Add the correct punctuation (full stops,
     commas) and appropriate conjunctions (but, when, and) to make a
     mixture of simple, compound and complex sentences.**

I felt very nervous as I opened the gates _____ started to walk up the drive
even though I had an appointment I was certain there was no one at
home _____ I got closer to the house it seemed even emptier the windows
looked out like blind eyes _____ the only sound was of my feet on the
drive _____ I reached the front door I had almost decided to turn
around _____ suddenly the door opened a large man loomed up over
me slowly beckoning me inside.

5.   **Now write a short paragraph describing the hallway of the house.**

_____

_____

_____

_____

_____

_____

_____

Check you have used the following:

☐ a simple sentence for effect

☐ compound and complex sentences

☐ descriptive detail using a subclause marked off with commas.

Writing your own description

You are going to combine all the different skills and techniques you have covered in this chapter into one descriptive piece called 'The Journey to School'.

Perhaps you walk to school or travel by car or bus. Perhaps you cycle. It doesn't matter – what matters is that you focus on *describing* so that the reader has a clear picture of your daily journey: what you see, hear, smell, touch. How it feels.

1. First, gather your ideas, drawing a spider diagram on a separate piece of paper. If you travel to school by bus, you might include details such as those in the spider diagram below.

leaving home:
waiting for the bus – how does it feel?
the bus stop

changing landscape through the window:
suburban streets, trees > busier as get closer to city
the traffic: smoky fumes

The Journey to School

senses:
scratchy seats, the noise of passengers talking, bus jolting over potholes

the people inside the bus – the driver, other students
some familiar faces – the old man with his hat: where is he going?

2. Once you have your ideas, you need to order them into a paragraph plan, like the one below. Make your own plan on a separate piece of paper.

Paragraph	What to include
1	Introduction – leaving the house and waiting at the bus stop (how does it look?)
2	How the bus feels
3	Time to look around – the people
4	…

Your order should make sense, and your paragraphs should focus on description, not on telling a story.

3.

a Once you've finished planning, think about how you will catch your reader's attention with description right from the start. Compare the two openings below.

> **A** I open the door and walk down the road. There are nice trees all along the road. At the bus stop, I usually have to wait for five minutes until the bus arrives. If I'm late, I have to run so I don't miss it, which is not good.

The sentences are clear and accurate, but there is no descriptive detail or precise vocabulary to give the reader a sense of how it feels to be on the journey.

> **B** The door slams behind me. If I'm on time, I amble along, breathing in the scent of the blossoms that line the street. But if I'm late, then I'm running so hard that my legs are on fire by the time I reach the bus stop with seconds to spare!

b What has Student B done to create a picture in your mind? Underline and label the key techniques: precise vocabulary, varied sentences, descriptive detail, the senses.

4. **You're ready to go. Write your description on a separate piece of paper (remembering the title: 'My Journey to School').**

As you write, use the checklist below to make sure you've included the key features of descriptive writing. Use it again when you've finished to check your work.

Precise vocabulary	
Use of the senses	
Use of imagery and symbols	
Variety and length of sentences: • simple • compound • complex	
Range of punctuation	
Clearly focused paragraphs	
Range of paragraph lengths for effect	

Responding to a descriptive text

Exploring the text

The passage below is from the opening of the poet and writer Laurie Lee's autobiography (published in 1959). Here he describes his arrival in the English countryside at the age of three.

The June grass, amongst which I stood, was taller than I was, and I wept. I had never been so close to grass before. It towered above me and all around me, each blade tattooed with tiger-skins of sunlight. It was knife-edged, dark, and a wicked green, thick as a forest and alive with grasshoppers that chirped and chattered and   5
leapt through the air like monkeys.

I was lost and didn't know where to move. A tropic heat oozed up from the ground, **rank** with sharp odours of roots and nettles. Snow-clouds of **elder**-blossom banked in the sky, showering upon me the fumes and flakes of their sweet and giddy suffocation. High   10
overhead ran frenzied **larks**, screaming, as though the sky were tearing apart.

For the first time in my life I was out of the sight of humans. For the first time in my life I was alone in a world whose behaviour I could neither predict nor fathom: a world of birds that squealed, of plants   15
that stank, of insects that sprang about without warning. I was lost and I did not expect to be found again. I put back my head and howled, and the sun hit me smartly on the face, like a bully.

> **Vocabulary**
> **rank:** reeking, stinking
> **elder:** a tree with strong-smelling white blossoms
> **larks:** songbirds

1. Explore the text by:

a reading it through carefully and getting a sense of the atmosphere Laurie Lee has created

b rereading and annotating each paragraph separately with a word or two to summarise the mood of that paragraph

c underlining, in each paragraph, the descriptive words or phrases that create that atmosphere.

2. Using three adjectives, summarise Laurie Lee's feelings in the passage.

Understanding the text

3. Answer the following questions to show your understanding of what is happening.

a At what time of year does Lee arrive in the countryside?

_____

b What is the weather like?

_____

c Why does he get lost so quickly?

_____

d Name three things that scare him.

_____

e What does he do when he realises he is lost?

_____

4. Now read the following statements and tick the one you agree with most.

a Because it is his first time in the countryside, Lee is excited to discover all the new things around him. ☐

b Because he has left his home in the town, Lee is desperate to go back there. ☐

c Because it is his first time in the countryside, Lee is terrified by the new things around him. ☐

5. Laurie Lee was three years old when he moved to the countryside; how might this be relevant to the description above?

_____

_____

_____

_____

Looking at the text in detail

6. ▶ **Focus on how Lee creates atmosphere.**

a In paragraph 1, find and write down *two* words or phrases that make the grass sound dangerous.

_____

b Lee compares grasshoppers to monkeys in paragraph 1. Write down *two* things this might tell you about them.

_____

_____

c Circle the two senses that Lee emphasises in paragraph 2.

| sight | touch | hearing | smell | taste |

For each one, find and write down a descriptive detail linked to it.

i _____

ii _____

d Lee repeats a phrase in paragraph 3. What is the phrase?

_____

e What is the effect of repeating this phrase?

_____

_____

7. ▶ **Complete the table below.**

Quotation	Effect
	makes the grass sound like a predatory animal, stalking him as prey
'the fumes and flakes of their sweet and giddy suffocation'	
'hit me smartly on the face, like a bully'	

Writing about the text

8. Complete the following task on a separate piece of paper, using the frame below.

> How does Laurie Lee describe the countryside from a child's point of view?

Laurie Lee uses some details to show how big everything looks to a small child. For instance, when he describes the grass, he says
He also describes the surrounding wildlife as if it were dangerous, unlike most people's idea of the English countryside. He writes that
In addition, he makes the sun and weather sound heavy and oppressive by
The effect of this description on the reader is to

Now read the end of the passage, where Lee describes his sisters.

> Faces of rose, familiar, living; huge shining faces hung up like shields between me and the sky [...]. They leaned over me – one, two, three – their mouths smeared with red currants and their hands dripping with juice.

9. Do you think this sounds like their little brother felt totally safe again? Circle your choice and explain your answer below.

> completely safe   mostly relieved   still a bit nervous   pretty terrified

Why? _____

_____

Thinking about the text

10. Did Laurie Lee succeed in making you feel what it was like for him as a child, moving home? Circle your choice.

> completely   mostly   more or less   a bit   not at all

11. Have you ever felt lost in a new place or a different environment? Reflect on this and note down some thoughts.

_____

_____

What is informative writing?

Read the following extract from an information text.

The Himalayas

The Himalayas are found in Asia, the world's largest continent in both size and population.

Geological Giants

The Himalayas are the largest mountain range on the planet. What makes them so huge?

1 Stretching for 2,400 km.

2 More than 50 million inhabitants.

3 Containing over 50 peaks more than 7,200 m high.

4 Home to the world's highest mountain, Mount Everest.

And, amazingly, they are still growing – by around 5 mm every year!

1. Label the following features on the text.

a main heading

b subheading

c image

d numbered points

e introduction

2.

a Which age group do you think this text would be most suitable for? Think about the style and language used, the amount of information given and the image. Circle your answer.

adults   young children   teenagers

b Why do you think that?

_____

_____

Identifying relevant information

Informative texts contain facts – information that can be checked and verified – to support the main ideas.

1. Look back at the text from Workbook Unit 2.2. List *two* facts that the writer uses to show that the Himalayas are the largest mountain range in the world.

a   _____

b   _____

Often, however, informative texts combine facts and opinions.

2. Read this extract from a newspaper article, then summarise *three* facts about visitors to the Himalayas in bullet points below.

> Every year, more and more climbers come to the Himalayas, perhaps hoping to reach Everest Base Camp; every year, many of them discover this is no simple task, and are hospitalised. These visitors blight the landscape, and the amount of rubbish collected by local guides is increasing annually. Everest, the world's largest and most majestic peak, is drowning under a sea of tourists. 'We can't deal with this for much longer,' said one local, who wished to remain anonymous.

_____

_____

_____

Opinions may be signalled by the following features:

> judgement adjective   speech   exaggeration
> uncertainty/possibility

3. Look at these opinions contained in the article. Label each opinion with a feature from the list above, and underline the relevant language feature.

a   'perhaps hoping to reach Everest Base Camp': _____

b   'world's largest and most majestic peak': _____

c   'drowning under a sea of tourists': _____

d   '"We can't deal with this for much longer," said one local': _____

Identifying bias

• •

'Asia is the largest continent' is a *fact*, but 'Asia is the most vibrant continent' is an *opinion*. The word 'vibrant' creates a *positive bias*, implying that Asia has a lively and creative energy.

Look at the underlined words in the sentences below.

> These visitors <u>blight</u> the landscape, and the amount of rubbish collected by local guides is increasing annually. Everest, the world's largest and most <u>majestic</u> peak, is drowning under a sea of tourists.

1. Complete the table below. You will need to identify another word with bias for the final row.

Word	Positive or negative bias?	Impact on reader
'blight'		implies
'majestic'		

2. Now look at these three headlines and draw lines to match them to the most likely impact.

a Too Many Students Fail to Reach Expected Levels   Neutral: informing of facts

b 42% Pass Rate in This Year's Final Exams   Bias: negative towards students

c Exams Failing Young People   Bias: positive towards students

3. Below are two newspaper headlines. What bias (if any) would you expect to find in each article, and why?

a **Rise in Electricity Charges Hits Families Hard!**

_____

_____

b **President Resigns Following Investigation**

_____

_____

Selecting and summarising information

Read the following passage about deforestation.

In many parts of the world, significant areas of forest are disappearing every year in order to clear land for farming. In the Amazon rainforest, for instance, deforestation can be seen from space.

One major consequence of deforestation is the loss of biodiversity: the rich plant-life of the rainforest is replaced by a single crop, such as palm (for oil). The loss of such diverse habitats dramatically affects the wildlife living there, including micro-organisms such as fungi, which keep the ecosystem healthy. 1 in 10 of the planet's known species are found in the Amazon rainforest, but many are now endangered.

Deforestation also affects humans. While new roads and farms may support local development, they also contribute to soil erosion. Tree roots provide 'anchors' for the earth, keeping rich topsoil in place; without them, rain washes away soil more easily, making the ground less fertile, and increasing the risk of floods and landslides. On a global scale, trees play a major part in absorbing carbon dioxide from the atmosphere; with fewer trees, the risk of global warming rises.

1. Now look at this task about the text above. Circle the words that tell you the focus of the task.

> Write a summary about the effects of deforestation.

2. Which of the following points are relevant to the task? Tick the points.

a Deforestation can support development through new roads. ☐

b Deforestation can be caused by farming. ☐

c 1 in 10 of the world's species are found in the Amazon. ☐

3. Here are two points from paragraph 2 that are relevant to the task and could be combined.

- 'One <u>major consequence</u> of deforestation is <u>the loss of</u> biodiversity.'

- '<u>1 in 10</u> of the <u>planet's</u> known species <u>are found in</u> the Amazon rainforest, but <u>many</u> are now <u>endangered</u>.'

In a summary, the sentences should be rewritten using your own words. For instance, the first sentence in could be rewritten as: *Deforestation leads to less biodiversity*.

a Rewrite the second sentence, changing the underlined words.

_____

_____

b Now combine both points, using a linking word such as 'and' or 'so'.

_____

_____

4. Go back to paragraphs 2 and 3 and underline relevant points relating to the task. Decide which can be combined (as in Question 3b) and then write them up in summary form below, making sure you change the wording as needed.

_____

_____

_____

_____

_____

_____

_____

_____

_____

_____

_____

_____

_____

_____

_____

_____

Developing presentation skills

Read the opening of a speech below. It is intended for younger students at your school, with the aim of encouraging them to improve the school environment.

> I'm here to galvanise you to take more care of the school environment. There are so many factors involved in this – producing less food waste, clearing rubbish from the grounds, making sure lights are extinguished – that it can seem like a daunting task. Some students will, inevitably, get more involved than others, leading to feelings of resentment towards those who are seen as not contributing.

1. The language is quite complex for younger students. Underline the words you would consider changing for this audience.

2. As well as some difficult vocabulary, the structure is also complicated, with long, complex sentences.

a Look at the following structural and presentation features. Number the features in order of importance for making the speech easier for younger students to follow.

☐ varied tone of voice   ☐ visuals

☐ shorter sentences   ☐ simple sentences

☐ more pauses   ☐ audience participation

b The speech ends on a negative note. How could this be changed to make younger students more likely to get involved?

_____

_____

_____

c Now write a new introduction that is clearer and more engaging for younger students.

_____

_____

_____

_____

_____

_____

Planning information texts to suit different audiences

....

1.

a Read the following extracts labelled A–D. Match each extract to the most likely audience below and write the extract letter (A–D) in the box.

[ ] formal academic   [ ] aimed at older readers

[ ] aimed at children   [ ] informal, among friends

b Underline the features that gave you a 'clue' as to the audience, such as vocabulary, sentence length and layout.

A

Puddings in plastic pots, fizzy drinks with straws and packets of crisps may be yummy, but they're not very good for you *or* the environment.

- Not much of the packaging can be recycled or reused.
- They often contain palm-oil.

B

Since I've been finding out more about the blue whale, I've discovered jaw-dropping facts: enough to make even the hardest-hearted cry.

So every year, whales are caught in fishing nets and actually drown – can you believe it?

C

Our research suggests that the walrus population is dwindling annually as a consequence of global warming. At the moment, we are monitoring several pairs in order to track their habits and rates of reproduction.

D

The World Wide Web has grown since its inception in 1989 to become the most common means of finding and communicating information. This has been particularly useful for those struggling to publicise environmental issues.

2. Extracts A–D are all types of informative text (spoken or written). What do you think each one might be?

A _____

B _____

C _____

D _____

3. Look at the following phrases, taken from extracts A–D. Put them in the appropriate column in the table below, and give an alternative version for one of the other audiences.

'jaw-dropping facts: enough to make even the hardest-hearted cry'
'since its inception'   'dwindling annually as a consequence of'
'packets of crisps may be yummy'

Formal	Informal
'since its inception'	since it started/began

4. Do you agree with the following statements? Put a ✓ to agree, ✗ to disagree, ? if you're unsure.

a It's all right to use informal language in certain situations, for instance, among friends. ☐

b I would always use formal language in any writing. ☐

c People often form opinions about others based on the way they speak or write. ☐

d Language is always changing. ☐

5. Look at extract E, from a school dining hall poster.

a Underline the features that show it is clearly aimed at teenagers.

b Imagine you are designing a similar poster for an office canteen. Rewrite it, focusing on changing the language you underlined in the first poster, but making sure you convey the same information.

E

Kids –

Every time you take the easy route and buy that can of the fizzy stuff, you're wrecking poor old Planet Earth! Each can is one more thing to recycle.

So, do your teeth and the planet a favour – bring your own water bottle.

Cheers!

Using direct and indirect speech to inform

1. Read the following passage. Underline the direct speech and highlight the indirect speech.

> Young environmental activitists caused a stir this morning, gluing themselves to the road to protest against rising pollution levels. They said they intended to stay there until the government agreed to consider banning diesel cars. 'It's our generation who will bear the brunt of all this driving,' said Leila Neto, one of the group. Passers-by were sympathetic, but a number of drivers who had been delayed were not so friendly. 'Get back to school!' shouted a waiting taxi driver. A spokesperson for the transport minister said that the government was already working hard to combat pollution.

2. Rewrite the following sentences with the correct punctuation.

a the head of Greenpeace praised the group for their courage saying our young people are the future

_____

_____

b it's really frustrating said Jonas we cant get the benefits of driving but we suffer the consequences

_____

_____

c one of the parents of the children who watched nearby said he was proud of his daughter

_____

_____

3. Turn these sentences into their 'opposite' (indirect to direct speech, or direct to indirect speech).

a 'It's true that we're holding up traffic,' said Leila, 'but if that's what it takes, so be it.'

_____

_____

b An angry commuter said that the environment was very important, but so was her job.

_____

_____

Planning an online news report

Read this opening of a news article.

> Jaheim Baker, 19, is not the first person to set up a community garden in the city, but he is the first to include beehives and a hedgehog refuge. 'I wanted to make sure there was a space for wildlife, not just humans, even in the city,' Jaheim explained. So how did a 19-year-old, who'd never had a garden before, and who spends most of his time working hard for his degree in Business Studies, end up keeping bees?

1.

a Which of the following sentences would make a better introduction or 'standfirst'?

> **A** A university student from Luongo, Angola, has turned a derelict building in his neighbourhood into a thriving eco hub.
>
> **B** Not everyone makes time in their lives for gardening, even though the benefits are proven.

b Why did you pick the one you did?

_____

_____

2. **Here is the plan for the rest of the article. Choose a connective from the bank below and write an opening sentence for each of the four paragraphs.**

However	But	Even so,	Last year	Some time ago	
Gradually	At first	Slowly	In the end	Finally	To sum up

Paragraph plan	Opening sentence
How Jaheim got the idea	
How he went about setting it up	
Things he's found difficult along the way	
Conclusion	

Writing your own informative text

Your school has decided to create a 'Learning Garden', to help students learn about the environment and to grow vegetables for school meals. You are going to write two texts informing students and parents about the new garden:

A a poster for classrooms informing students about what the garden will do and how they can contribute

B an article for the school newsletter informing parents about the new garden, and why it is important.

1. **First, plan your ideas about the learning garden in a spider diagram. You could use the one below as a starting point, adding your own ideas.**

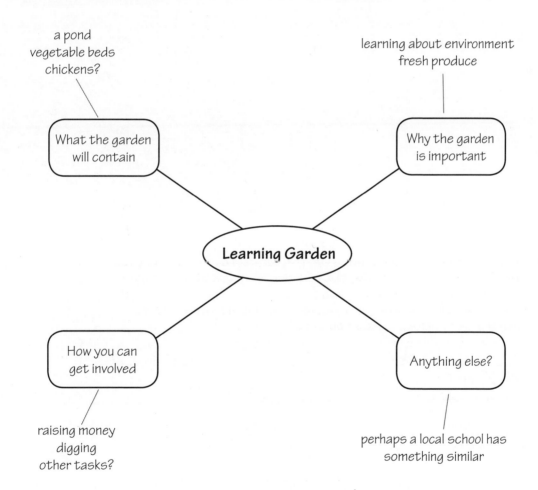

a pond
vegetable beds
chickens?

learning about environment
fresh produce

What the garden will contain

Why the garden is important

Learning Garden

How you can get involved

Anything else?

raising money
digging
other tasks?

perhaps a local school has something similar

2. Now you have gathered ideas, you need to plan how you will present this information to different audiences, in different formats. Use the Venn diagram below to note key features, using some of the ideas below and adding your own.

| subheadings | specific terminology (environment) | | formal tone | bullet points |
| images | clear paragraphs | | text boxes | clear, engaging vocabulary |

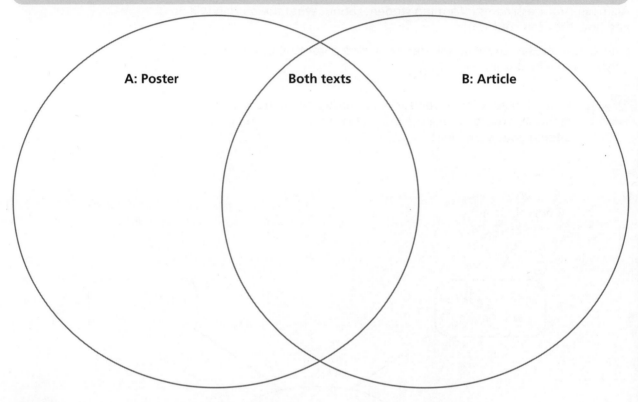

A: Poster   Both texts   B: Article

3. Now organise your ideas into a clear structure. For the article, you will need to use paragraphs, but your poster might include boxes with information. You might also put different information in each text, depending on what your audience would be interested in. Use the table below to help you plan.

Poster	Article
Heading – main text?	Introduction
Information box 1	Paragraph 1
Information box 2	Paragraph 2
Information box 3	Paragraph 3
	Conclusion

4. Now write up your two texts on separate pieces of paper. As well as checking grammar and spelling, check levels of formality, using the Venn diagram to help you.

Responding to an informative text

Exploring the text

Read this article about environmental campaigners.

Direct Action is Back

The environmental movement is on the march again, but this time, it's not just adults – children are taking their future into their own hands and making some serious statements.

Almost 50 years ago, Greenpeace, one of the world's foremost environmental charities, was founded in response to growing fears over nuclear weapons. Since then, it has broadened its focus, with campaigns ranging from fossil fuels to deforestation, from **GM** crops to whale hunting. Their policy of '**direct action**' has brought them into conflict with governments around the world.   10

5

A new generation

Today, however, it is the grandchildren of the Greenpeace generation who are taking to the streets in direct action of their own. Greta Thunberg skipped school to start her now-famous Friday School Climate Strike in 2018. What started with one courageous 15-year-   15
old, sitting alone on the street with a handmade sign, is now a global movement, as students walk out of schools around the world, from Uganda to Japan, in protest at adults' inaction.

As with Greenpeace, there are supporters and detractors. Thunberg's own father has described his mixed feelings about his daughter's   20
actions but, in the end, he says, 'She can either sit at home and be really unhappy, or protest, and be happy.' Critics may argue that children cannot understand global politics, but how many of them have won a Nobel Peace Prize nomination?

Meanwhile, the students keep on marching. Whatever the grown-   25
ups believe, they prefer Thunberg's view: no one is too small to make a difference.

Vocabulary

GM: genetically modified

direct action: taking action, such as protest, rather than simply stating disagreement

1. **Explore the text by:**

- underlining any factual information the writer uses to make her point
- circling any words or phrases that indicate a bias on the writer's part.

Understanding the text

2. **Based on your reading, are the statements below true or false? Correct the false ones.**

a Greenpeace was founded in response to rising sea levels.

_____

b Greenpeace favours direct action, which makes it unpopular with some people.

_____

c Young climate strikers are the direct descendants of the founders of Greenpeace.

_____

d Students have taken part in protests all around the world.

_____

e Greta Thunberg's father took her to her first climate strike protest.

_____

f Criticism from older people has made students realise they are wrong and should stay in school.

_____

3. **The writer has included some important facts in her article to inform the reader about the development of environmental action. Complete the summary below, using the relevant facts from the text.**

Greenpeace was founded in 1971, to protest against _____

The group expanded to other issues, for instance _____

Sometimes, they have got into trouble because of _____

The first youth climate strike started with _____

in _____

Since then, _____

Adults have _____ feelings about the students striking.

_____

4. ▶ **Circle your answer. Do you think the writer supports:**

a Greenpeace? Yes / No / A bit / Not sure

b the school strikes? Yes / No / A bit / Not sure

Looking at the text in detail

5. ▶

a Find a phrase in paragraph 1 that suggests students are independent.

_____

b Find a word in paragraph 2 that suggests Greenpeace is important.

_____

6. ▶ **Now look at paragraph 3 and complete the table below.**

Words or phrases	Effect
'courageous 15-year-old, sitting alone'	
	She sounds like she doesn't have much, but has made an effort all the same, like she really cares.
'adults' inaction'	

7. ▶ **Using the words from the box below, complete this response to the writer's use of direct and indirect speech.**

indirect   wrong   supportive   the students   question

In the article, Greta Thunberg's father is quoted as saying his daughter will be unhappy if she doesn't strike. This makes him sound like a _____ father, because he allows his daughter to choose.

However, when the writer mentioned the students' critics, she uses _____ speech, and she follows it with a _____ . This has the effect of making the readers focus back onto _____ and makes the critics seem _____ .

Writing about the text

8. | How does the writer present information to suggest that the students are right?

Use the scaffold to help your write your response.

The writer begins by suggesting how important groups like Greenpeace have been. She says that
When she first presents Greta Thunberg, she makes her sound quite different to powerful adult campaigners, by describing
However, she goes on to suggest that, like Greenpeace, the students have attracted criticism, for instance
Ultimately, the writer undermines criticism by

Thinking about the text

9. | **Reflect on this question and make a few notes below.**

Do you agree that 'No one is too small to make a difference'?

_____

What is writing to advise and persuade?

1. Circle the best answer(s) to the following questions.

a What is persuasive writing?

  i   a way to help readers do something correctly

  ii a way to influence a reader's opinion

  iii a way to make people do things

  iv all of the above

b What is advice writing?

  i   guidance on how to do something

  ii a story about someone who helped you

  iii suggestions for how you can improve something

  iv all of the above

2. Persuasive writing uses persuasive adjectives. Underline the positive adjectives in sentences a–d, then explain below why they are persuasive. The first one has been done for you.

a Our Wildlife Café serves <u>wholesome</u> food for all the family.

Effect: <u>Suggests it is tasty and healthy.</u>

b Watch our dolphins do incredible tricks and wow the audience with their clever antics.

Effect: _____

c Learn about conservation by watching our fascinating films.

Effect: _____

d The souvenir shop has some memorable gifts for friends and family.

Effect: _____

3. Persuasive writing also uses adverb-adjective combinations, for example, 'breathtakingly close'. Add the strongest adverbs from the box below to fill the spaces in this advert.

> very   stunningly   utterly   really   brilliantly   stupidly   shockingly

> The wildlife sanctuary includes _____ beautiful tropical zones for a range of parrots and exotic birds. Prepare to be _____ captivated by the birds-of-paradise and the _____ clever myna bird, which imitates human voices.

4. What overall impression do you get of the sanctuary now that these adverbs have been added?

_____

5. Underline at least *three* suggested 'dos' and 'don'ts' in the following text.

> Never go into the lion enclosure. However, if you do, make sure it isn't feeding time. Otherwise this could end up being a rather unpleasant experience for you. If the lion looks hungry, you should run away as quickly as you can. Don't bother to take any photos or you might end up with a selfie that isn't very pleasant.

6. What is the main purpose of the text in Question 5? How do you know?

_____

_____

7. Modal verbs are used in a range of ways in advisory and persuasive texts:

- necessity or obligation: *must, ought, should*
- certainty: *will*
- possibility: *might, may, could*
- ability: *can.*

Circle any of these modal verbs in the text in Question 6.

8. Write the missing modal verbs in this advice text.

> If you find an injured bird in your garden, you _____ phone the National Society for the Protection of Birds, who _____ advise you on what to do next. You _____ nurse the bird back to health, if it is not too badly hurt, but you _____ be clear about what to do.

9. Write the first three sentences of either an advice text or an advert from a travel company about seeing tigers in the wild.

Advice text: While you are travelling in our special trucks, do not	Advert: Join us on our amazing tiger adventure and see these
_____	_____
_____	_____
_____	_____
_____	_____

Making inferences from persuasive texts

1. Complete the following sentences, using words from the box below.

less obvious   literal   meanings   hinting

a Words can be read in more than one way: they have explicit and implicit _____.

b The explicit meaning is the _____ meaning of a word: this is the most basic or usual meaning.

c However, words also have an implicit meaning, which is _____; this is something the writer is _____ at, but not necessarily saying in a straightforward way.

Look at this sentence.

The airline has <u>rigid</u> baggage rules, so make sure you check your bags carefully before leaving.

The sentence literally means that the airline has strict rules about baggage – this is explicit.

But it *hints* that the airline won't change or bend these rules under any circumstances ('rigid' means unbending) – this is implicit.

2. Now look at the underlined words in the sentences below. For each sentence, circle the correct implicit meaning.

a The hotel stands <u>head-and-shoulders</u> above any other.

   i It's very high.

   ii It's better than all the others.

   iii It has a statue on the top.

b Come and sample the <u>mouthwatering</u> selection of dishes in our restaurant.

   i The food is very spicy.

   ii The food will make you salivate.

   iii The food is delicious.

c The film brought audiences <u>to their feet</u> at the end.

   i It was so good, they stood to applaud.

   ii It was so bad, they walked out.

   iii They needed to stretch their legs.

3. The extract below is from a persuasive article about circuses.

> For some people, the prospect of going to the circus makes them want to dance; for others, like me, the thought alone brings tears to my eyes. We should all be asking ourselves why we want to see a majestic elephant kneeling before the ringmaster or forced to stand on one trembling leg, simply for our amusement.

a How does the writer feel about circuses?

_____

_____

b Which phrase hints at how the writer feels in the first sentence?

_____

c Now look at the second sentence. Match the meanings from the box below to the words from the extract and write them in the table.

> bowing   shaking   treated like a servant   frightened

Word	Explicit meaning	Implicit meaning
'majestic'	royal	deserving respect
'kneeling'		
'trembling'		

d The writer tries to persuade the reader that elephants should not be treated in this way by using words that have powerful implied meanings. Complete these sentences to explain how. You can use words from the table above to help.

The writer describes the elephant as if it is a _____.

This makes us feel it is _____.

However, the writer also suggests the elephant is suffering by telling the reader that _____

_____.

Using quotations as evidence

Using quotations is important because they give evidence to support your personal response to a piece of writing.

1. Quotations should be precise. Tick the response below that has a more precise quotation.

The writer says, 'We should all be asking ourselves why we want to see a majestic elephant' being treated this way. This implies the elephant deserves respect. ☐

The writer describes the elephant as 'majestic', which implies it is powerful and deserves respect. ☐

2. Quotations should also be correctly punctuated, with quotation marks around the words from the text. Add quotation marks to the sentences below (referring to the passage in Workbook Unit 3.3 for guidance).

a The writer says the elephant is kneeling before the ringmaster, almost as if it were a servant.

b The writer implies that animals should not be made to perform simply for our amusement.

Now complete this sentence about the passage using one, precise quotation, correctly punctuated.

c The writer suggests that the experience makes her sad by saying

_____

Read the passage below.

Our donkey rides provide a safe and fun environment for children to enjoy close contact with animals. All our donkeys are used to even the tiniest tots, and our expert handlers are always close by to guide and support, leaving you free to stand back and capture the magical experience on camera!

3. Underline all the positive adjectives in the passage that the writer has used.

4. Using the adjectives that you underlined in Question 3 as quotations, answer the question below.

How does the writer persuade parents that their children will be safe on the donkeys?

_____

_____

Speaking to discuss and to persuade

Read the conversation between three students below, and then answer the questions that follow.

Ana: So, my family is going to the circus this weekend, and my mum asked if I wanted to invite you.

Chang: I wouldn't go to a circus if my life depended on it.

Ana: Why not? It'll be fun: the poster says it's the most mind-blowing circus experience you'll ever have! You should give it a chance, don't you think?

Chang: I have – my uncle took us to one last year, and there were cats jumping through flaming hoops, and I found it heart-breaking: imagine how terrifying for those cats! It's just not right to make animals perform like that.

Ana: Oh, I hadn't thought of it that way – still, we've already bought tickets. Are you abso–

Chang: I said, no. Thanks, but no thanks.

Suze: Ok – I get what you're saying, Chang, and no one wants to see animals hurt, but Ana has already got tickets. What's more, I hear this circus has a humane approach to animals. Maybe we should give it a go?

1. **Identify the places where the following discussion skills or errors occur in the conversation by highlighting the text and adding the relevant letter beside each example.**

a using positive adjectives to persuade

b interrupting someone else

c asking questions

d using a personal anecdote

e using exaggerated language

f summarising different ideas

2.

a Who do you find more persuasive – Ana or Chang? Why?

_____

_____

_____

b Which student do you think listened best, and why?

_____

_____

_____

c How did Suze develop the discussion sensitively?

_____

_____

3. ➤ Both Ana and Chang are writing speeches to present to the class, for and against circuses. Below is Chang's plan, in the form of a spider diagram.

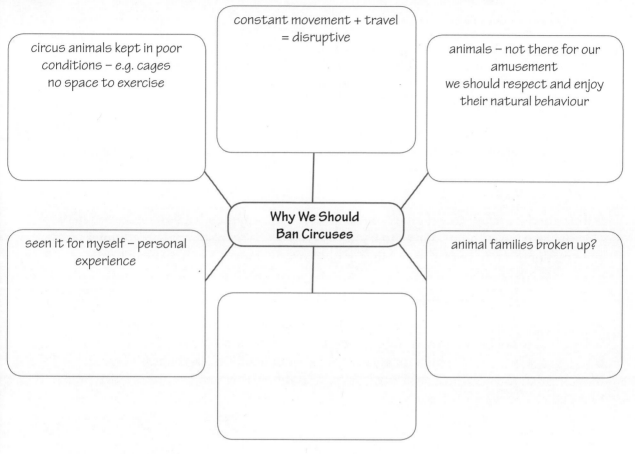

circus animals kept in poor conditions – e.g. cages no space to exercise

constant movement + travel = disruptive

animals – not there for our amusement
we should respect and enjoy their natural behaviour

Why We Should Ban Circuses

seen it for myself – personal experience

animal families broken up?

Help Chang structure his speech to create the most persuasive effect.

a Number the ideas 1 to 6 (including one new point of your own) so that he can write the speech in a logical order.

b Include persuasive language by writing one word or phrase he could use next to each section. For example, next to 'animal families broken up?', you might write 'cruel separation' or 'family unit destroyed'.

c How could Chang make his speech even more persuasive for his audience? Think about how he could use his voice and what he could show to support his presentation.

He could include _____

When speaking, he could_____

_____

_____

Structuring an effective advice text

Advice texts need to be clear and organised in order to be useful. The
following extract is from an advice text about looking after younger children.
It has been written in paragraphs but is missing other organisational
features, such as subheadings and connectives to link ideas.

Looking after younger children can be great fun, but it needs a bit of planning: it is
important they are given activities to do that match their specific age, needs and interests.

_____

If they are close in age to you, they may enjoy similar games and activities, so you may
already have ideas and resources to hand. You can probably also remember things you
enjoyed doing a few years ago, so dig out old toys and books you may have kept!

_____

a _____, preschool-age children present more of a challenge. They
will probably not be used to sitting still and listening, so don't expect them to!
b _____, plan for a variety of shorter activities, perhaps involving
movement or music, with clear instructions. And if they don't enjoy what you've prepared,
don't take offence.

_____

For all the activities you plan, ask yourself if they are age-appropriate. Will some
children be scared by a television programme you love? Will they understand the rules
of a complicated game? If you're unsure, it's always worth checking with parents or
carers beforehand.

_____

c _____, your priority must always be keeping the children in your care –
and yourself – safe. You may enjoy cooking, or cycling along the road, but young children
are unlikely to have much awareness of risk. Don't attempt anything potentially dangerous.

d _____, if you remember these
simple guidelines – plan suitable activities and
always put safety first – the experience is likely
to be rewarding not only for them, but also
for you.

1. When you have read the text carefully, insert connectives from the box below into spaces a–d in the text, so that the ideas are clearly linked.

instead   in the end   most importantly   however

2. Adding subheadings to signal the focus of each section would make the text easier to read. Allocate a suitable subheading for each paragraph from the list below and write it in the space provided in the text.

What is appropriate?   Activities for younger children
Safety first   Activities for school-age children

3. Make a paragraph plan for an advice text of your own, using the frame below (you can use more than one paragraph for each section if you wish). It could be about looking after a bike, caring for plants, or preparing to give an important speech – you choose!

What to include	Paragraph number(s)	Topic/content	Subheading
The benefits			
Guidance with examples			
Potential problems			
Solutions			
Summarise in a positive way			

Using complex sentences to develop ideas

Adverbs and expanded or additional phrases can be used to add detail to simple sentences.

1. Draw an arrow from each underlined part of this sentence to connect it with the correct grammatical term beneath.

The <u>wolves</u> <u>ran</u> <u>silently</u> <u>through the woods</u>.

adverb   noun   additional phrase   verb

2. Complete the chart below to create more detailed sentences. Some have been done for you.

Noun	Verb	Adverb	Additional phrase
The children	played		in the street.
Rabbits	scampered		
		softly	
	plodded		
The birds			

Moving around sections of a sentence adds variety to your sentence structures, but also emphasises different words. Compare the different effect of these two sentences: *Through the wood, the wolves ran silently* and *Silently, the wolves ran through the woods.*

3. Rearrange three of the sentences from your chart in Question 2 to create new sentences with a different focus and effect.

a _____

b _____

c _____

You can build detail and interest in your writing by using complex sentences, as well as simple sentences.

4.

a Draw arrows to connect parts of this sentence with the correct terms beneath.

Although they are generally peaceful creatures, gorillas are very protective of their young.

comma to separate ideas   main idea   supporting idea   linking word

b Which of the following linking words or phrases could you use to replace the one in the sentence above? You should keep the meaning the same.

because   while   as   even though   however

Read this opening to a persuasive extract.

Throughout the world, humans are steadily destroying animal habitats. [1] Even though it is too late for some species, there is still time to save others. [2] All hope is not lost. [3]

5. **Match each sentence in the extract to an effect below, writing the sentence number next to the effect.**

a Provides a change of tone: _____

b Implies a more positive outlook: _____

c Emphasises the negative: _____

6.

a Now write your own persuasive opening to a text entitled 'Animal Racing Must Stop Now!' using a variety of sentences for different effects. You could move from positive to negative, or vice versa.

_____

_____

_____

_____

b Now check your work, using the checklist below.

Did you:

☐ use a simple sentence for effect?

☐ build up detail with an additional phrase?

☐ create a different tone with a complex sentence?

Writing your own persuasive letter

Read the following task.

> Write a letter to your head teacher persuading them to support an endangered species as the school's next charity.

1. You need to plan your letter clearly. Use this space to note down your ideas.

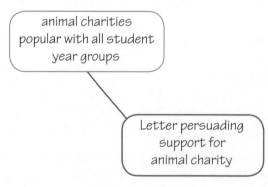

animal charities popular with all student year groups

Letter persuading support for animal charity

2. Now organise your ideas into a clear order. You can use a table or make a flowchart like the one below.

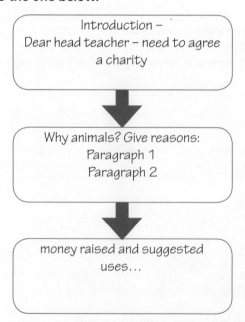

Introduction –
Dear head teacher – need to agree a charity

Why animals? Give reasons:
Paragraph 1
Paragraph 2

money raised and suggested uses...

3. Once you are happy with the content of your plan, write up your letter on a separate piece of paper. Remember to set it out like a letter, with your address and the date in the top right-hand corner.

You can also use suggested words and phrases from the bank below to help you.

> **Persuasive words and phrases suggesting dangers**
> catastrophe   disaster   tragedy   emergency   destroy
> decimate   engulf   erode   close to extinction
> vulnerable   defenceless

> **Persuasive words and phrases suggesting solutions**
> glimmer of hope   beacon   lifeline   citizenship
> stewardship   responsibility   restore   care for
> nurture   protect   pledge   life-saving   committed

> Your address
>
> Date
>
> Recipient's address
>
> Dear …
> …
> …
> …
>
> Yours sincerely,
> …

Formal language appropriate to purpose and audience		
Clear paragraphs (including introduction and conclusion) Range of connective phrases		
Variety of sentence structures	simple	
	compound	
	complex	
Features of persuasive writing	powerful and relevant facts	
	persuasive opinions	
	powerful word choices	

Use the checklist as you write to make sure you include persuasive features. Use it again to check your work when finished.

Responding to a persuasive text

Read this extract from a speech about endangered species.

Earth – our planet – our home, is made up of more than a million different species of animals, birds and insects. This may seem like a massive number and you may think that it is not important if some animals die out. However, this biodiversity is vital to our everyday lives. It is the link that joins all living things together, and if it is broken it could seriously make it difficult for us to get enough food. I strongly believe that our environment has reached a moment of crisis. 5

All scientists and biologists agree that it is humans who have caused this crisis. In the last few decades, our use of Earth's natural resources has skyrocketed faster than our planet can provide, and there are signs that the number of species becoming extinct is increasing very quickly. 10

There are over 16,300 animals on the endangered species list and I'd like to look in more detail at just one of them. The most endangered big cat at the moment is the Amur leopard, in my opinion, one of the most gorgeous animals on our planet. There are only about 100 left in the wild. Tragically, because of their fabulous coat, they have been hunted illegally. It makes me absolutely furious when I learn of animals killed in this way. I think that these 15 hunters should be punished with many years in prison.

I have no doubt that if we continue like this there will be a major world disaster. This could happen during our own lifetime if we do not act immediately.

Exploring the text

1. **Explore the text by:**

- highlighting any sentences or phrases where you think the writer expresses a strong personal view (for example, 'I strongly believe')

- underlining any factual information the writer uses to make their point

- circling any powerful adjectives or adverb-adjective combinations that make animals seem wonderful

- picking out any other phrases or sentences that help persuade the reader.

Understanding the text

2. According to the speech extract, are the following statements true or false? Correct the false ones on the lines beneath.

a There are more than a million different species of animals and fish on the planet.   T / F

_____

b It's not important that some animals become extinct.   T / F

_____

c Biodiversity is the link that joins all living things together.   T / F

_____

d We are using less of the world's natural resources than previously.   T / F

_____

e Any disaster will happen a long time in the future.   T / F

_____

f We need to act immediately.   T / F

_____

g There are only about 100 Amur leopards left alive in the world.   T / F

_____

h The leopard is hunted for its coat.   T / F

_____

3. Which of the following statements best summarises the writer's opinion? This means the statement that sums up the overall view, not just one part of their opinion. Tick your answer.

a She is only concerned about saving the Amur leopard. ☐

b She is extremely concerned about all animals under threat of extinction. ☐

c She isn't concerned about animals under threat. ☐

d She wants stronger punishments for hunters. ☐

Looking at the text in detail

4.

a Find a word in paragraph 1 which suggests that the world is in a serious situation.

_____

b Find a word in paragraph 3 that shows how sad the writer is at what is happening to the leopards.

_____

5. **Look more closely at paragraph 3. Find and write down the following:**

a a simple sentence for shock effect

_____

b a complex sentence that begins with an adverb for emphasis.

_____

6. **Complete the table below by writing in the following:**

a the persuasive technique used (powerful verb, data as evidence, use of personal pronoun)

b the effect intended.

Quotation from the text	Technique and effect
'Earth – our planet – our home' (line 1)	
'use of Earth's natural resources has skyrocketed' (line 8)	
'over 16,300 animals on the endangered species list' (line 11)	

Writing about the text

7. | How does the writer try to persuade the reader that she is right about extinction of species?

Use this scaffold to write your answer.

The writer makes some really important points about why we should worry about extinction. For example, she states that
She also sounds very persuasive because she uses emotional or powerful statements such as
In addition, she makes the reader care about the Amur leopard when she calls it   The effect of this is
She ends the speech with a warning by telling the reader that

Thinking about the text

8. | What do you think? Do you agree with the writer of the speech – or are you more hopeful? Circle your answer.

completely disagree   partly disagree   partly agree   completely agree

Write a sentence explaining your views.

I think that _____

Exploring mystery and suspense narratives

. . . .

1. How do you choose the stories or books you read? Tick any boxes that apply (there are no right or wrong answers).

Friend recommends it. ☐

Browse in a bookshop. ☐

Browse in a library. ☐

Teacher recommends it. ☐

Parent recommends it. ☐

Read a review about it online or in a magazine. ☐

See a film, then want to read the book. ☐

Other (_____) ☐

2. What was the last book you chose to read? Write a sentence saying why you chose it.

I chose _____

_____

3. Draw lines to match these features of suspense stories to their definitions.

1 obstacle   **a** build-up of mystery and uncertainty

2 climax   **b** character's purpose or motive

3 resolution   **c** moment of highest emotion/drama

4 tension   **d** questions or mysteries answered or worked out

5 goal   **e** problem to be overcome

4. Use your own ideas to complete this suspense structure, starting with a character's goal. (Continue on a separate piece of paper if you don't have enough space.)

Goal: Amal wants to find out about her new mysterious neighbour...

Obstacle: _____

_____

_____

_____

Understanding how story openings work

Read this opening to a suspense story, which starts in the middle of the action.

Amal quietly crept through the overgrown dusty yard towards the back door. Would it be open? Was anyone in? She had seen the strange man leave the house, but what if he'd come back without her realising? She slowly turned the door handle…yes, it opened! She was in. She used her phone's torchlight and looked around the room. It was like a school science lab. There was a complicated set of glass containers bubbling with liquid, and long tubes with a weird purple mixture in them. What on earth was it? She was just about to take a photo when she heard them: footsteps coming up the path! She looked desperately for somewhere to hide, but there was nowhere. The handle turned, and a figure stepped into the light…

1. Highlight the use of any question marks, exclamation marks and ellipses in the passage.

2. Now write down from the passage:

a one question that shows Amal's uncertainty

_____

b one question that shows Amal's fear of being discovered

_____

c one question that shows her trying to make sense of what is happening

_____

d one sentence that uses an exclamation mark to show her relief

_____

e one sentence that uses an exclamation mark to show shock or fear

_____

f one sentence that uses an ellipsis to create a cliffhanger (where readers ask themselves, *what's going to happen next?*)

_____

3. On a separate piece of paper, write a paragraph commenting on how the writer has used punctuation to create suspense. Use your ideas from Question 2. For example:

The writer uses question marks to show how uncertain Amal is, for example when …

Exploring how writers create characters

Read this passage about two rather unusual-looking characters from a story called 'The Tall Woman and her Short Husband'.

> She was seventeen centimetres taller than he.
>
> One point seven five metres in height, she towered above most of her sex like a crane over chickens. Her husband, a bare 1.58 metres, had been nicknamed Shorty at college. He came up to her earlobes but actually looked two heads shorter.
>
> And take their appearances. She seemed dried up and scrawny with a face like an unvarnished ping-pong bat. [...] Her husband on the other hand seemed a rubber **rolypoly**: well-fleshed, solid and radiant. Everything about him – his calves, insteps, lips, nose and fingers – were like pudgy little meatballs. He had soft skin and a fine **complexion** shining with excess fat and ruddy because of all the red blood in his veins. His eyes were like two high-voltage little light bulbs, while his wife's were like glazed marbles. The two of them just did not match, and formed a marked contrast. But they were inseparable.
>
> from 'The Tall Woman and her Short Husband' by Feng Ji-Cai

Vocabulary

rolypoly: someone of round, plump appearance

complexion: colour or texture of the skin on a person's face

1. **List five things the writer tells us explicitly about the man.**

a His height:_____

b His skin:_____

c The colour of his face:_____

d His eyes:_____

e His overall appearance:_____

2. **What simile does Feng Ji-Cai use to describe the appearance of the woman's eyes?**

_____

3. **What does this simile suggest about the woman's character – or how she might behave?**

_____

4. Feng Ji-Cai says that the woman has 'a face like an unvarnished ping-pong bat'.

Why is this an effective simile?
Write a sentence.

This is *effective because* _____

_____

5. The writer uses the image 'rubber rolypoly' to describe the man and the simile 'like an unvarnished ping-pong bat' to describe the woman's face.

What ideas come to mind when you read these descriptions? Add your ideas to the diagrams below.

bouncy, round

'rubber rolypoly'

'unvarnished ping-pong bat'

6. What is the surprising statement the writer makes about the husband and wife at the end of the extract? Find the quotation from the passage and write it here.

_____

7. What impression is given of the man from the passage? Choose then tick one of these statements.

a The man is described in a comical and amusing way. ☐

b The man is described sympathetically. ☐

c The man is described as rather disgusting and not pleasant to be with. ☐

d The man is described as very frightening and threatening. ☐

e Your own, different view. ☐

8. On a separate piece of paper, write a paragraph supporting your view.

Using role-play to understand character

Read the following speech from a play with a hidden mystery.

> *Saj (alone) enters a room in his grandfather's house. He looks around slowly, then stops.*
>
> **Saj:** Those tiles – there's something strange about them. Let me take a closer look. The pattern doesn't match…
>
> *Saj pushes, and suddenly the 'wall' slides back.*
>
> What? You're kidding! I mean I knew my grandfather had secrets, but this is WEIRD.
>
> *He steps inside the hidden room.*
>
> Maps. Lots of them. And what's this? An old suitcase with… passports, clothes, unopened tins of food. The passports are of children – here are their pictures! And bus and train tickets. Lots of tickets.
>
> What can it mean? Grandfather lived through the war, but he said he just kept out of trouble while the enemy occupied the city. Somehow I don't think he was telling the truth. But I can't ask him, can I? If he'd wanted me to know, he'd have told me. Wouldn't he?
>
> *Suddenly, there's a sound.*
>
> Oh no! He's coming upstairs. What am I going to do?

1. **How would you play the role of Saj? Prepare this script for a performance.**

a Put a / for a place where you might pause – for example, while thinking.

b Underline any words or phrases you want to say with force or emphasis.

c Add an up arrow (↑) for where you might need to make your tone go up (for example, at the end of a question) and a down arrow (↓) for down.

d Make a note at the side of any lines where a gesture or movement (such as shutting the suitcase suddenly) might be needed.

2. **How might you use your voice, facial expression or movement to show the suspense and tension at the end of the scene? Add a note saying what you would do.**

_____

_____

3. **What do you think Saj's grandfather was doing in the war? Write a sentence or two in explanation.**

_____

_____

Planning and structuring your own story opening

1. Read this summary of the beginning and middle of a suspense story. Where would you begin the story to have the biggest impact on the reader?

> Two friends set out in a boat to do some fishing. But the weather turns stormy. They are forced to head for a cave under some cliffs, but the storm batters the boat and they have to jump in and swim. They find safety in the cave but the waters rise and they are trapped.

I would start with the moment when_____

because_____

2. Now fill in the following flow diagram to complete the story structure you have chosen. Remember: if you start with a dramatic moment, you can still add further exciting events. You will need to add your own ideas, such as the ending.

> Opening

> The story develops

> The dramatic climax!

> Tension drops slightly

> Resolution – for good or bad!

3. Write your opening paragraph on a separate piece of paper. Remember to capture the reader's interest. Make sure you *show* what is happening – for example, describe how 'he grabbed the slippery rock desperately', rather than just tell the reader 'he was desperate'.

Introducing your own characters

Clear, accurate punctuation and grammar can really help when you create characters in suspense stories.

1. **Identify the mistakes in this story version of the script from Workbook Unit 4.5. Circle or underline the error and say what needs to be done. The first one has been done for you.**

Sentences	Error or change needed
a Saj looked at the tile pattern there was something very strange about it.	The comma needs replacing with a semicolon: *Saj looked at the tile pattern; there was something very strange about it.*
b He pushed the wall suddenly it slid back	
c 'What. You're kidding me, he said out loud.	
d Inside the room the walls were covered in maps charts newspaper cuttings and faded photos of children.	
e Saj shook his head slowly. Why had his grandfather kept all this stuff hidden for so long.	
f Out of the blue, there was a noise it sounded like his grandfather coming up the stairs.	

2. **Imagine you have drafted a conversation between Saj and his grandfather from earlier in your story.**

As Saj entered the kitchen his grandfather was stooping over the stove stirring a pan of rice he didn't look up as Saj came in but just continued with what he was doing Why won't you talk to me about the war asked Saj touching his grandfather on the shoulder Some things are better left alone his grandfather growled.

You've forgotten the punctuation! Rewrite the draft on a separate piece of paper, adding in the correct punctuation.

You can add detail to character descriptions by expanding phrases or parts of sentences.

3. **Add detail to the following paragraph. In each case, use the suggested type of word/phrase listed below.**

(1) adjectives   (2) adverb   (3) conjunction

a   Saj's grandfather had _____, _____ (1) hair, which didn't get combed very often.

b   Often, he would just sit _____ (2) in his old chair, watching the television.

c   _____ (3), today Saj saw that his hands were shaking and he wasn't really taking any notice of the TV.

d   Saj decided to open the shutters_____ (3) that light flooded in, _____ (3) his grandfather didn't seem at all pleased.

4. **Using compound and complex sentences can help to add character detail. Taking these simple sentences as a starting point, add your own detail to turn them into compound or complex sentences. Use the suggested conjunctions. In some cases, these can be moved to the front of the sentence.**

a   Saj loved his grandfather (even though/although/yet)

_____

b   His grandfather drank his mint tea (while)

_____

c   It was clear his grandfather had some bad memories (because/as)

_____

5. **On a separate piece of paper, write your own opening paragraph introducing a mysterious older character. Here are some ideas:**

a   someone who lives alone in the wild

b   a storyteller or performer in a marketplace

c   an IT specialist who spends long hours on his/her laptop.

Writing your own suspense narrative

You are going to write a story full of suspense, with interesting characters.

The title will be: 'Lost on the Mountain'.

Your story could be about someone (or more than one person) on a hiking or climbing trip when it suddenly gets very foggy or snowy and they can't find their way down.

Stage 1: Generate ideas

Use the spider diagram below or your own way of making notes.

Who are the characters?

Where? Time of year? Weather?

Lost on the Mountain

What happens? How does it end?

Who is telling the story? Is it in the first or third person?

Stage 2: Sum up your story using this timeline

Put obstacles/problems under the line, and the 'good' parts above it.

The climb begins

Stage 3: Gather vocabulary and check your spelling

Read this bank of useful words for your story. Add at least *five* more of your own. Check your spelling. Most of these words are nouns. Could you change any of these nouns to adjectives (for example, 'rock' to 'rocky')? Add some adjectives, adverbs and verbs.

rocks	boulders	glacier	balance	crevasse	summit
control	rope	edge	despair	escape	precipice
descent	ascent	fall	speed	distance	foothold

Stage 4: Write your story

You will need to write your story on a separate piece of paper.

Remember:

- Show, don't tell!
- Make your main characters interesting through speech, physical description, and so on.
- Include exciting moments when the reader doesn't know what will happen.
- Use punctuation and sentences creatively to create surprise, tension or drama.

Stage 5: Evaluate

Now, think about how successful your story was. Complete the sentences below.

(a) One good thing about my story: _____

_____

(b) Something I need to improve: _____

_____

Responding to a mystery and suspense story opening

Read the opening to this mystery story, then answer the questions.

The Little Shop of Curious Objects

Surely he had lost them? Javed breathlessly turned a corner and dived into the first shop he came to. The gang of bullies wouldn't follow him in here, would they? He glanced anxiously out of the shop window, but it was a quiet street and no one passed by. In fact, now he thought about it, this street was one he'd never seen before. He turned around,   5
ready to make his excuses to the shopkeeper and leave. But there was no one there.

He began to take in his surroundings. At the back of the shop was a dusty counter with an old-fashioned till. The shelves around the shop were bending under the weight of the junk crammed onto them: broken ornaments, toys with missing parts, single shoes, grimy bottles with faded labels.   10

Suddenly, a strange figure emerged from the gloom behind the counter, almost as if it had been there all the time. It was an old woman, wearing a stained apron. She had piercing blue eyes and a thin nose, like a hawk's as it looks at its prey, and her laser-beam stare seemed to focus on Javed.

'So, you've come for the job?' she croaked, her voice hardly more than a whisper.   15

'Job?' said Javed, bemused. 'Er… I'm not sure I…'.

'It's time someone took over the shop,' she interrupted. 'Here, you can start by putting this on a shelf for me.'

She reached under the counter and handed Javed an object. It was a human skull.

The old woman grinned, 'Don't worry, young man, it won't bite. After all, it is two   20
hundred years old.'

By Mike Gould

Exploring the text

1. **Explore the text by:**

a underlining any factual information the writer tells us about either Javed or the shopkeeper

b highlighting any words or phrases that create a strong image

c circling any phrases or sentences that suggest mystery or strangeness

d picking out any other phrases or sentences that help make the opening vivid and mysterious.

Understanding the text

2. **Which of the following statements about the story opening are true? Rewrite the false ones with the correct information underneath.**

a Javed was being chased by bullies. T/F

_____

b The shop he entered was on a busy street that he knew well. T/F

_____

c The shop was full of old or useless items. T/F

_____

d The shopkeeper avoided Javed's gaze. T/F

_____

e When the shopkeeper spoke, it was difficult to hear her. T/F

_____

f The shopkeeper immediately offered him a job. T/F

_____

g She asked Javed to put a human skull on the shelf. T/F

_____

h The skull was over three hundred years old. T/F

_____

3. **In your opinion, which of the following is the most mysterious aspect of the story?**

a The woman has an old skull in the shop.

b Javed had never seen the street the shop was on before.

c The old woman offered him a job.

d The shop is full of useless junk.

Looking at the text in detail

4. Find the following words or phrases in the text and write them in the spaces provided.

a An adverb in the first paragraph that means 'in a worried way'.

_____

b Two adjectives in the second paragraph that describe ways in which items or parts of the shop are unclean or uncared for.

_____ and _____

c A verb in the third paragraph that means to look at someone in a very direct way.

_____

d An adjective that describes Javed's confusion when the woman offers him a job.

_____

e A verb describing how the woman smiles after she gives Javed the skull.

_____

5. The writer uses similes and metaphors in the passage. Explain in your own words what each of the following suggests.

a 'like a hawk's as it looks at its prey'

This suggests that the woman stares at Javed as if _____

_____

b 'laser-beam stare'

This suggests the woman's stare is _____

_____

The writer shows Javed's feelings in different ways.

6. What two questions does he ask himself in the first paragraph?

a _____

b _____

7. What examples of ellipses can you find in the conversation?

_____

8. What do these uses of language tell us about how he feels?

These show the reader that _____

Writing about the text

9. **How does the writer make this story opening interesting and mysterious?**

Use this scaffold to write your answer.

The writer uses lots of techniques to make the story interesting and mysterious, such as
In particular, at the start, we don't know what has happened because
The shop itself is rather mysterious because
The old woman is strange in a number of ways. Firstly, she is described as being Later, what she says creates mystery when

Thinking about the text

10. **What do you think might happen next? Will the woman turn out to be good or bad? Circle your choice below.**

Really terrible   Slightly bad   Neither good or bad   Slightly good   Very kind

Write a sentence explaining your views.

I think that_____

Exploring how playscripts convey character and action

Read the following extract from a play based on *Jane Eyre* by Charlotte Brontë. Jane has been forced to leave the house where she was working. She comes to a remote village and sees two young women through the window of a cottage.

Rain. Jane knocks at the door. An older woman, Hannah, a servant holding a candle, answers.

Hannah: (*surprised to see someone outside*) What do you want?

Jane: (*shivering*) May I speak to the mistresses of the house?

Hannah: You had better tell me what you have to say to them. Where do you come from?

Jane: I… I am a stranger.

Hannah: What is your business here at this hour?

Jane: I simply want a night's shelter in an out-house or anywhere, and a morsel of bread to eat.

Hannah: (*distrustfully*) I'll give you a piece of bread but we can't take in a vagrant.

Jane: Please let me speak to your mistresses. I beg you!

Hannah: No. Your wandering about looks very suspicious to me.

Jane: But where shall I go if you drive me away? What shall I do?

Hannah: Here is a penny; now go—

Jane: (*sinks to her knees*) A penny cannot feed me, and I have no strength to go farther. Don't shut the door:—oh, don't, for goodness sake!

1. **What are your first impressions of Jane and Hannah? Write any adjectives you can think of into the two profile heads below.**

Jane

Hannah

2. **Now answer these questions about the script.**

a Note down at least three pieces of evidence that tell the audience it is night-time.

1 _____

2 _____

3 _____

b What two stage directions tell us that Jane is weak and suffering?

1 _____

2 _____

c What two words suggest that Hannah thinks Jane is trying to trick or steal from the house?

The first is a stage direction that describes how Hannah speaks.

1 _____

The second is an adjective Hannah uses to describe Jane walking around at that time of night.

2 _____

3. **A student has begun to write up their impressions of Jane. Fill in the missing information.**

It is clear from the stage directions that Jane is suffering, as it states she is '_____' when she asks to speak to the 'mistresses of the house'. At the end of the scene, when she is offered a '_____' by Hannah, it describes how she '_____ to her knees'. She must be starving because she tells Hannah that '_____'

_____

4. **Write a paragraph about Hannah, commenting on how she is presented.**

Begin: In this scene, Hannah is presented as someone who is_____

_____

_____

_____

_____

_____

_____

Discussing and developing ideas for your own plays

Read the following discussion between five students. They are planning a short play about an outsider.

> **Rex:** So, my idea is about a boy from the big city. He moves to the countryside, but finds it boring and quiet…
>
> **Anita:** Yes. That makes a good contrast. Because he's used to the noise and bustle, but suddenly he's an outsider surrounded by nature, but he hates the smells (*laughs*)
>
> **Jamal:** But…
>
> **Anita:** (*ignoring him and continuing*) So, he could have this massive argument with his parents and try to go back to the city.
>
> **Rex:** Great – that sounds good. And his parents realise they've made a big mistake and move back.
>
> **Jamal:** Yes, but that sounds a bit unrealistic, doesn't it?
>
> **Rex/Anita:** (*together*) No – it's totally realistic.
>
> **Jamal:** But wouldn't it be more interesting if, like, his opinion begins to change? He begins to appreciate the natural world. Meets local people. What do you think, Mel?
>
> **Melody:** Yes, that's a good idea, Jamal. He could perhaps meet another boy, his own age, and…
>
> **Rex:** (*interrupting*) No, we've got a great idea – we don't need to discuss it any more.
>
> **Seb:** Can I just say something?
>
> **Anita:** No – we've discussed it – let's get acting!

1. How did the discussion go? Write the names of each of the students into the boxes below.

Says the original idea is the best	Says the original idea could be developed in a different way	Doesn't get the chance to say what their idea is

2. Now, read these statements about discussion skills or mistakes, and draw lines to match them to the speaker or speakers.

1 interrupts someone

2 ignores someone

3 praises someone

4 asks someone what they think

a Anita

b Jamal

c Rex

d Melody

3. It is clear that some members of the group were not good at turn-taking! Which of these phrases would be best to use to make sure everyone in the group gets a chance to speak? Tick your choices.

a What do you think, Seb? ☐

b Shut up everyone! ☐

c Have you got any ideas or comments? ☐

d So, what you're saying is…? ☐

e That's interesting – tell us more. ☐

f You're too shy. Speak up, then we'll listen. ☐

4. Write a paragraph about your group discussion skills here.

I think I am good at_____

However, I think I could improve by_____

_____

_____

_____

_____

_____

_____

_____

_____

_____

Performing and scripting plays

Read the following monologue. It is based on the situation from Workbook Unit 5.3 about a boy moving to the countryside from the big city.

> **Jem:** (*holding phone*) Is that you, Priya? Sorry, what's that? (*pause*) I can't hear you very well – the signal is terrible here! I'm sorry if it cuts off suddenly. Anyway, I thought I'd call to tell you about my amazingly exciting life now we've moved to the middle of nowhere. (*pause*) No – I'm being *sarcastic*. There is literally NOTHING going on here. It's great if you like birdsong, nice views and goats, goats and more goats – *lots* of them. Can't you hear them? *Meuh, meuh, meuh!* That's what wakes me up every morning. No! It's not sweet. It's … annoying. I never thought I'd miss the sound of cars, streetlights keeping me awake, or our old, cramped flat. But I do!

1. **What tone of voice do you think Jem would use? Tick one or more options.**

a angry ☐

b happy ☐

c fed up ☐

d hopeful ☐

e cruel ☐

2. **Write one sentence explaining why you think this.**

I think Jem's tone of voice would be_____ because

_____

3. **When do you think Priya speaks?**

a Put a 'P' in the script where you think she speaks, for example, *Is that you, Priya? P Sorry, what's that?*

b Make a note of what Priya might be saying, for example, *Yes, Jem, it's me!*

4. How would you read Jem's monologue aloud? You will need to imagine Priya is listening.

a Underline any clues already in the speech that will help you read it aloud (for example, the 'pause' instruction or punctuation marks).

b Highlight any words or phrases you could stress or emphasise.

5. Now develop Jem's character. What else might he say about being in the countryside? Complete this second part of his monologue.

Jem: Another thing I really miss is _____

I used to love _____

I suppose one good thing about being here is _____

However, I am worried about _____

What if I don't _____?

6. Now, read the whole monologue (the original plus yours) as one full speech. You could perform it to a friend or relative, or record it and then play it back.

7. Use this grid to evaluate your own performance. Write a comment in the first column and then tick the appropriate box.

Skill/technique	Needs work	Getting there	Got it!
clarity and fluency			
tone and emphasis			
use of pace and pauses			

Exploring the structure of reviews

Read the following two paragraphs from a review of a film called
The Outsiders in a TV listings magazine.

The Outsiders directed by Francis Ford Coppola, 1983

Sat 8.15 p.m. Channel 14

Emotional teenage drama about kids from the wrong side of the tracks

The film *The Outsiders* is based on the bestselling novel by S.E. Hinton, which she wrote
when she was just 17. The film, which is set in the late 1960s, tells the story of a group
of teens (the 'Greasers') who are poor and who come into conflict with the richer youths
from another part of town. The film captures the time perfectly, and is extremely moving
and dramatic.

It also features many talented young stars who went on to become household names.
These include Tom Cruise and Patrick Swayze, but it is the convincing performances
of C. Thomas Howell in the lead role of Ponyboy and Ralph Macchio, as his best friend
Johnny, who steal the show.

1. What does each paragraph cover? Tick the correct box.

		Paragraph 1	Paragraph 2
a	the actors who became celebrities when they were older	☐	☐
b	the background to the film	☐	☐
c	the main plot	☐	☐
d	the acting skills of two of the cast	☐	☐
e	the overall mood of the film	☐	☐

2. Find the positive adjectives in the review based on these
definitions.

a heartfelt _____

b exciting _____

c gifted _____

d believable _____

3. What do each of these idioms, used in the review, mean?
Tick the closest explanation in each case.

a 'captures the time'

i gives a truthful impression of the era ☐

ii prevents people from escaping ☐

iii goes into the future successfully ☐

b 'household names'

i the names of houses ☐

ii known by ordinary people ☐

iii names of actors ☐

c 'steal the show'

i make a surprising impact ☐

ii ruin the film ☐

iii make the plot interesting ☐

4. Here is another paragraph from the review.

Howell is excellent as the youngest brother of three in a family orphaned when their parents were killed in a car crash. He clashes with the eldest brother, Darrel (Swayze), who is trying to keep him from getting into trouble. Macchio is equally good as a younger, wild, but frightened boy whose parents are always fighting.

a Which part of the review does the extract above come from –
before, *between* or *after* the two paragraphs you read on page 78?
Circle your answer.

before   between   after

b How do you know?

I know because_____

_____

5. How else does the reviewer show they are still positive about the film? Underline any further positive adjectives.

Developing the language of reviews

1. The following words all come from a review of the novel of *The Outsiders*. Circle the one that is spelled correctly in each case.

a character   chariter   caracter   charactor

b atmosfear   atmosphere   atmusphere   atmospher

c narrater   narator   narrattor   narrator

d protaganist   prottagonist   protagoniste   protagonist

e dialogue   dialog   diealogue   dyalogue

2. Look at this image of Ponyboy (left) and Johnny (right) from the film *The Outsiders*.

light-coloured denim jacket

Annotate the image with as many details as you can, using vocabulary as precisely as possible.

3. Now, read this further paragraph from the review that appears in Workbook Unit 5.5, commenting on Macchio (the actor who plays Johnny). Fill in the gaps with your own information, using the image above. Try to be precise in the vocabulary you choose.

Macchio certainly looks the part in his _____ jacket with the turned-up _____.

His _____ hair and the _____ look in his eyes, definitely fit the idea of a troubled teenager. Howell is _____ than Macchio and that also suits the idea of him being older than his friend.

4. The following sentences all come from the same review of the film *The Outsiders*.

- In each case, circle or underline any errors or areas for improvement (for example, in the use of tenses).
- Write the improved version underneath.

a 'In one scene, Ponyboy and Johnny went to a drive-in movie and met these two rich girls.'

_____

b 'Darrel Ponyboy's older brother has to do several jobs to keep the family together.'

_____

c 'A key turning point in the plot is the seen when the boys turn heros during a fire at an abandoned church.'

_____

d 'Francis Ford Coppolas most famous film is probably *The Godfather*, it starred Marlon Brando.'

_____

e 'Although released in 1983, the film still feels relevent today and of interest to modern audiances.'

_____

Now read this paragraph of a review of a very different piece – a humorous play.

My Classmate is a Robot is quite a funny play about a human boy, Jed, who goes to school on another planet. Although he is an outsider, he soon makes friends with a robot in his class, and the two have a few adventures together. The friendship between Jed and the robot is quite moving and the acting is quite believable.

5. Can you make the paragraph stronger and more positive? Replace weak words or phrases with more powerful ones from the word bank below. Rewrite the paragraph on a separate piece of paper.

hilarious   countless   very emotional   totally convincing

Writing your own review

Read these three short extracts from reviews of plays or films on the theme of the outsider.

A

Twelfth Night is a play full of outsiders. The shipwrecked twins, Viola and Sebastian, have to survive in a strange land while dealing with the possibility that their twin has drowned. Viola does this by disguising herself, and this leads to a lot of comedy, but I felt sympathy for her.

B

Every great story needs a good villain, and Gaston in *Beauty and the Beast* is perfect. Played brilliantly in this production by Tom Smith, he has a sneering voice and is always flexing his muscles, showing off his strength. When he fights the Beast the audience boo and hiss, which is exactly what any director wants.

C

The setting of 60s Oklahoma is perfectly recreated by Coppola. The windswept parking lots and empty playgrounds, as well as the low houses with their porches and screen-doors, really take the viewer into that world.

1. Tick the extract or extracts that comment on:

		A	B	C
a	one particular actor and his skills	☐	☐	☐
b	the location and how believable it is	☐	☐	☐
c	how the play/film begins – its main story	☐	☐	☐
d	the reaction of the viewer/audience	☐	☐	☐
e	different emotions that are created.	☐	☐	☐

2. Each extract A–C above follows a similar structure: Topic sentence – Evidence (detail to support the main point) – Audience reaction.

Using a different colour, highlight the different parts of each extract, and put **T**, **E** and **A** alongside them.

3. Now choose any recent play or film you have seen and plan your own review of it.

Stage 1: Choose your film/play

Make notes about your chosen film/play, using these headings:

- Plot/storyline: who, what, where
- Acting: names or type of role (e.g. hero, villain, sidekick)
- Production details: setting, locations, costumes, design
- My opinion

Stage 2: Plan your review

Use this structure to help you plan.

Introductory paragraph	Main details – title, director, a little bit about the plot/storyline and style
Paragraph 2	First focus – e.g. the plot
Paragraph 3	Second focus – e.g. the performances
Paragraph 4	Third focus – e.g. the production
Concluding paragraph	My overall opinion/audience response

Stage 3: Draft your review

On a separate piece of paper, draft your review. You may wish to use this word bank.

production	cast	character	hero/heroine
villain	dramatic	comic	humorous
moving	scene	set	design
performance	impact	audience	reaction
recommend	show	staging	action
plot	climax	relationship	sympathy
sequel	director	tragedy	journey

Checklist for success

✔ Use the present tense.

✔ Include a brief summary of the plot, but not the ending.

✔ Include your own viewpoint through use of positive or negative adverbs and adjectives.

Responding to a scene from a play

• •

Read the following scene from later in the play *My Classmate is a Robot*.

In this scene, A4 (the robot) is showing Jed around his new school.

> *JED and A4 enter a large space where there is a set of sunloungers.*
>
> **JED:** So – this is the playground, then? On Earth ours has a basketball net and a shop where you can buy snacks.
>
> **A4:** Playground? How. Do you 'play' with the 'ground'?
>
> **JED:** Er – no. It means a place where students can play – run   5
> around, kick or throw a ball. Let off steam.
>
> **A4:** Steam? I understand. Like engine. Fuel.
>
> **JED:** No – it's just a saying. It means... oh, never mind. What is this place, then?
>
> **A4:** You run. On water. We have fuel, too.   10
>
> **JED:** (*slightly irritably*) We don't run on water, A4... well, actually, maybe we do – but not in the way you mean. Anyway, where were we?
>
> **A4:** In the. Classroom. Now, we are. Here.
>
> **JED:** (*groans*) I mean – what were we talking about?   15
>
> *A4 makes a whirring sound, and begins to slow down.*
>
> **A4:** (*low, slurred voice*) Need... Fu... u... el... now... www...
>
> **JED:** You sound awful, A4! Are you... err... ill? Do you need oiling... or something?
>
> **A4:** Help me. Must... sit... down.   20
>
> *JED looks at A4, and then eventually starts to push him towards one of the sunloungers. A4 zig-zags about a bit and then half-rolls onto a sunlounger.*
>
> **A4:** (*very quiet*) He... e... lp. Open. Puh... lease!
>
> *JED looks at A4 then realises he has a curved lid on his front. JED opens it, revealing a silvery foil panel. JED suddenly realises what is happening.*   25
>
> **JED:** Oh – I get it! *Fuel* – you run on solar power!

Exploring the text

1. **Explore the text by:**

a underlining any information the writer gives on the setting

b circling any guidance given on how the actors should speak or move

c highlighting any funny confusions or interesting moments in the drama.

Understanding the text

2. **Answer these questions about the script.**

a What items of furniture are in the robot-school playground?

_____

b What two things does Jed say can be found in his playground at his 'Earth' school?

_____

_____

3. **A4 misunderstands Jed several times.**

a What does he think 'playground' means?

_____

b A4 thinks that humans are powered by water. Which of Jed's phrases makes him think this?

_____

c When Jed says 'where were we?' what does he mean?

_____

4. **How does the audience know there is something wrong with A4? Give three pieces of evidence from the text.**

1 _____

2 _____

3 _____

5. **What are the sunloungers for?**

_____

Looking at the text in detail

6. **'Let off steam' is a common idiom in English. What does it mean? Circle your answer.**

a calm down

b release the energy inside you

c boil a kettle

d get really angry

7. **Tick the correct answer. If someone's voice is 'slurred', it is:**

a faster than usual ☐

b in a foreign language ☐

c slower, with words running into each other ☐

d very quiet, in a whisper. ☐

8. **When Jed says, 'We don't run on water… *well, actually, maybe we do*' – what is he saying? Tick your answer.**

a that people *can* actually 'run' on water – by swimming! ☐

b that it rains a lot on Earth ☐

c that we drink lots of water when we're running ☐

d that we can't survive without water, so it is a sort of fuel ☐

9. **Explain how the playwright shows how A4's voice is slurred through the way he:**

a spells 'Please'

He writes it as _____ which makes it sound

_____

b uses ellipses (…).

He uses ellipses when A4 says_____ to show that

_____

10. What bracketed stage directions show that Jed is finding the conversation difficult?

Example 1 _____

Example 2 _____

Writing about the text

11. How does the writer bring out the very different worlds of Jed and A4 in this script?

Use this scaffold to write your answer.

At the beginning, Jed and A4 have a different idea of what a 'playground' is. Jed
Another key area of confusion is when A4 misunderstands   This leads to a discussion about
A key difference is also shown by the writer when A4 begins to malfunction. This is shown through
Towards the end, Jed finally realises what the sunloungers are for when

Thinking about the text

12. What do you think might happen next? Will A4 recover? What other experiences might Jed face?

Write a sentence explaining your ideas.

I think that_____

_____

Exploring and commenting on a poem's language

Read this opening to the poem 'Snake' by D.H. Lawrence.

A snake came to my water-trough
On a hot, hot day, and I in **pyjamas** for the heat,
To drink there.

In the deep, strange-scented shade of the great dark **carob**
    tree
I came down the steps with my pitcher
And must wait, must stand and wait, for there he was at the
    trough before me.

He reached down from a fissure in the earth-wall in the
    gloom
And trailed his yellow-brown slackness soft-bellied down,
    over the edge of the stone trough
And rested his throat upon the stone bottom,
And where the water had dripped from the tap, in a small
    clearness,
He sipped with his straight mouth,
Softly drank through his straight gums, into his slack long
    body,
Silently.

From 'Snake' by D.H. Lawrence

> **Vocabulary**
>
> **pyjamas:** light clothes suitable for sleeping or wearing in the heat
>
> **carob:** a flowering, evergreen tree

 1.   **The poet describes a simple experience he has had.**

Complete this sentence summing it up.

The poet goes to get water because _____

There may be some words in the poem that you do not know but could work out from the grammar and the context of the sentence (the rest of the information around them).

The following is an example of how you could work out the meaning of a word.

Word: 'water-trough'

Grammar:

- 'trough' – it's a noun as it is the object of the sentence ('came to my water-trough')

- the use of the possessive pronoun 'my' tells us it belongs to the poet.

Context:

- other mentions of the 'trough': it has an 'edge'; it has a 'stone bottom'
- the snake has come 'to drink there'.

2. **What is a 'water-trough', based on this information? Tick your answer.**

a a phrase meaning 'to feel thirsty' ☐

b a type of tap made from stone ☐

c a stone container to hold water ☐

d a type of bucket that carries water ☐

3. **Using a similar approach to Question 2, write down the meanings of these words.**

a pitcher _____

b fissure _____

c slackness _____

4. **There are several repeated words or words linked to the same ideas.**

Complete the table below.

Words or phrases suggesting it is a warm day	Words or phrases suggesting the snake's thin, stretched-out appearance

5. **A student has started writing about the poem 'Snake'. Complete her paragraph about the poem.**

Lawrence explores the snake's shape and movement in several ways. For example, he suggests the snake stretches his body when he '_____ down' from the wall. He also describes the snake's body as '_____' and his _____ as 'straight'. This suggests _____

6. **How would you describe the overall 'feeling' or tone of the poem? Circle one of these options and write a paragraph explaining your answer.**

a fast and dramatic

b slow and thoughtful

c broken-up and confused

d loud and funny

I think the overall tone of the poem is_____

Exploring and commenting on a poem's form and structure

Read this short animal poem, then complete the tasks that follow.

A
    slimy
        squelchy
soft
    black
        slug…

Has eaten all my new-grown plants

And
    now is
        crawling on my
soft
    white
        rug!

Vocabulary
slug: a snail-like creature

1. Are these statements about the structure of the poem true or false? Circle the correct letter for each statement.

a The poem is made up of two main stanzas. T / F

b The last words of each stanza rhyme with each other. T / F

c The poem uses shape to reflect the subject. T / F

d The first stanza describes the white rug. T / F

e There are no repeated words in the poem. T / F

f The poem is made up of mostly one-word lines. T / F

g Each of the two main stanzas have the same number of lines. T / F

h The dividing line between the stanzas is longer than the others. T / F

2. Now complete this gap-fill paragraph about some of the patterns in the poem. Use the word bank below to help you.

> contrasts   black   rug   exclamation mark   disgusted   white

The poet _____ the slug with the _____
by saying one is 'soft' and '_____' while the other is
'soft' and '_____'. The use of the _____ at
the end of the poem emphasises how _____ he feels.

3. Write your own paragraph, discussing how the poet has used shape and structure. You could use this writing frame.

The poet uses the shape of the poem to represent…

This works well because you can visualise…

He also uses lots of single word lines which make you read the poem…

This is like the way in which a slug moves because…

_____

_____

_____

_____

_____

_____

_____

_____

_____

_____

_____

_____

_____

_____

Exploring and writing poems using non-standard forms

Wanted – crocodile feeder

Wanted – crocodile feeder
Experience essential
Long arms desirable
V good swimmer preferable
Totally unflappable
Must have life insurance

1. The poet uses another form of writing in this funny verse. What is it? Circle your answer.

a a letter

b a job advert

c a leaflet about crocodiles

d a playscript

2. How do you know? Write one sentence explaining the reasons for your answer to Question 1.

_____

One of the things about this form of writing is that it uses:

• abbreviations

• incomplete sentences – often phrases.

3. Write the text out in its full form on a separate piece of paper. It has been started for you below.

(We need/want) a crocodile feeder OR Do you want a job as a crocodile feeder?

(You) must have experience…

4. Write your own funny advert poem for a job with animals. Here are some suggestions.

hawk trainer   elephant cleaner/washer   lion tamer

Exploring and commenting on sound in poetry

1. Here are four types of sound devices used in poetry: assonance, onomatopoeia, sibilance and alliteration. Draw a line to match each term to its definition.

1 Assonance...

2 Onomatopoeia...

3 Sibilance...

4 Alliteration...

a ... is when a word copies or echoes a sound, for example, 'moan', 'murmur', 'whizz', 'clip-clop'.

b ... is a type of alliteration that creates a whooshing or hissing sound that matches the subject, for example, 'the sea spray sloshed on the stony shore'.

c ... is the repetition of initial consonants, for example, 'Peter Piper picked a peck of pickled peppers'.

d ... is the repetition of vowel sounds, for example, 'The ice did split with a thunder-fit'.

2. Now reread the following lines from the poem 'Snake' by D.H. Lawrence. As you read:

a underline the examples of sibilance

b circle the examples of assonance. (Slightly more difficult to spot!)

> He sipped with his straight mouth,
> Softly drank through his straight gums, into his slack long
>   body,
> Silently.

3. Why do you think the poet uses these sound effects?

I think the poet uses sibilance such as _____ and _____

because_____

Read this short verse about a sloth.

The Two-toed Sloth

It's not that he's dozy or dull or deliberately slow
He's just conserving energy, considering the leaves,
Cocooned in his comfy forest home, wondering...
Why he's got two toes when others have three?

4. On a separate piece of paper, write about the sound devices (including rhyme) used in the poem 'The Two-toed Sloth' and any effects they might have.

Exploring themes in poetry through talk

Read the opening of a poem below aloud.

Caged Tiger

Hey, Mummy, can we see the tiger, can we, can we?
We want to see it pounce and roar!
But Mummy knows the tiger's sleeping,
Knows the tiger hardly moves at all.

Hey, Mummy, why's the tiger hiding?
Is he just waiting to leap on his prey?
But Mummy knows the tiger's forgotten
All he learned as a cub at play.

1. **What do you notice about the way the poem is written?**

Answer these questions to help you decide.

a How many voices are there in the poem?

_____

b How does the poet show the difference between them?

_____

_____

2. **Which adjectives are most suitable to describe the tone of voice for the italicised speech (the first two lines of each stanza)?**

Circle adjectives from this word bank.

silly   excited   disappointed   angry   triumphant   cold   anxious

3. What do you think the theme of the poem is? Read this discussion between three students.

> **Bryn:** So, this is all about how kids are innocent – they don't understand things. Like when the line says, 'But Mummy knows the tiger's sleeping'. The children think it's more exciting.
>
> **Su:** I think it's more than that. The poem is called 'Caged Tiger', so perhaps it's more about zoos – locking animals up. Like it says, the mum knows the 'tiger hardly moves at all'. He doesn't move because he's not got anywhere to go.
>
> **Jade:** I think you're both right. They're young kids, right *(they call her 'Mummy')*? So, they probably don't understand things like habitat, so yeah – it's innocent. But the mum also says 'the tiger's forgotten all he learned as a cub at play' – that's because he's in a zoo and doesn't need to catch prey. It's not natural, is it?
>
> **Bryn:** I guess not.

4. Are these statements true or false? Circle the correct letter in each case.

a Bryn argues the poem is about how little children are innocent. T / F

b Jade doesn't agree with either of them. T / F

c Su completely disagrees with Bryn T / F

d Jade takes bits of both their arguments and adds to them. T / F

e Su partly agrees with Bryn. T / F

5. Who do you agree with? Do you think the students are right about the themes of the poem – or is the poem about more than this? Write your views below.

I think the poem is about how_____

_____

_____

_____

Introducing key points

· ·

1. **Read the following opening sentences commenting on the poem, 'Caged Tiger' from Workbook Unit 6.6. Each sentence could also be written using a colon or semicolon.**

Think about where a colon or semicolon would go, then rewrite the new sentence. You may need to change or remove some words.

a The child is excited to see the tiger and wants to see it 'pounce and roar'.

_____

b Children expect tigers to behave in particular ways, such as roaring, pouncing or leaping on their prey.

_____

c The mother knows the reality, while the children only see the fantasy.

_____

d The tiger in the poem is presented as being very passive, for example, it 'hardly moves' and has 'forgotten how to play.'

_____

2. **Complete this gap-fill task, adding any suitable connectives from the word bank below so that the paragraph is clear and makes sense.**

> however   as   initially   furthermore   but

_____, we hear the voice of a child who begs his mother to go and see the tiger.

_____, his mother knows it will be a disappointment _____ the tiger is behind bars and is usually 'sleeping'. _____ she realises that even when it is not asleep, it 'hardly moves at all', _____ she doesn't tell the children this.

3. **Write an opening sentence to the next paragraph about the children's views. Use at least one connective, colon or semicolon. You could start:**

The children pester their mother_____

Responding to an animal poem

Read the whole of the poem below and then complete the tasks that follow.

Caged Tiger

Hey, Mummy, can we see the tiger, can we, can we?
We want to see it pounce and roar!
But Mummy knows the tiger's sleeping,
Knows the tiger hardly moves at all.   5

Hey, Mummy, why's the tiger hiding, why, why?
Is he just waiting to leap on his prey?
But Mummy knows the tiger's forgotten
All he learned as a cub at play.

Hey, Mummy, Mummy, the tiger's boring!   10
Can we go and see the crocodile?
But Mummy just stands there sadly watching,
Says, *Let's just wait a little while.*

Hey, Mummy, Mummy, why are you crying?
The tiger's silly and stupid, not like in our books.   15
But Mummy's thinking of a trip to Sumatra,
Of a time long ago when she got her first look.

She's remembering the stealth, and the soft, soft footsteps,
She's remembering the glitter of those fierce, diamond eyes,
She's remembering the rippling coat glowing gold in the forest, 20
The menacing sight of those inky black stripes.

Time to go, she says finally, wiping tears with a sigh.
We'll come back tomorrow, or perhaps in a week.
Or perhaps never, she thinks, as they queue for the penguins,
Still sensing the salty smears on her cheek.   25

By Mike Gould

Exploring the text

1. **Explore the text by:**

a underlining any special or notable ways the poem is set out or presented on the page

b circling any strong descriptions of the tiger or the mother

c highlighting any notable uses of sound, rhyme or rhythm.

Understanding the text

Answer these questions about the poem.

2. **How do the children react to the tiger in the zoo? Tick *two* correct statements.**

a They are excited by how it leaps and roars. ☐

b They say the tiger is 'boring'. ☐

c They ask to go and see the crocodile. ☐

d They start crying like their mother. ☐

e They say it's similar to the tiger in their book. ☐

3. **List at least *two* features of the tiger that the mother remembers from visiting Sumatra.**

_____

_____

4. **What do the mother and the children do after they have been to see the tiger?**

_____

Looking at the text in detail

5. How does the poet convey the children's voices in the poem?
Tick any correct statements.

a The first two lines of most verses are in italics. ☐

b They repeat phrases again and again. ☐

c The poet gives their names and uses speech marks. ☐

d They use informal language. ☐

e They ask lots of questions. ☐

f Every other verse is spoken by the children. ☐

6. Give at least *two* quotations from the poem which show that the mother doesn't enjoy watching the tiger in the zoo.

_____

_____

7. Draw lines to match these sound techniques with examples from the poem.

1 'the rippling coat glowing gold'   **a** rhyme

2 'the stealth, and the soft, soft footsteps'   **b** assonance

3 'roar'   **c** alliteration/sibilance

4 'crocodile' / 'while'   **d** onomatopoeia

8. In the fifth verse, what two words tell us the mother thinks that wild tigers are precious?

_____ and

_____

9. What do the following lines tell us about how the mother feels about taking the children to the zoo again?

'We'll come back tomorrow, or perhaps in a week.
Or perhaps never'

_____

_____

Writing about the text

10. | How does the poet explore the theme of zoos in the poem?

Use this scaffold to write your answer.

The poet uses the two voices of the child or children and   This means the reader sees
The children's view of what a tiger should be like is shown through   This suggests they don't
The mother, on the other hand, sees the reality as she knows that   This shows
The mother's feelings are presented strongly in the poem by   At the end, we realise

Thinking about the text

11. | Do you think the mother will return with the children to the zoo?
Tick the box you think applies.

Definitely not ☐   Possibly ☐   Probably ☐   Definitely ☐

Write a sentence explaining your ideas.

I think that the mother will/will not _____

_____